FINDING, HIRING, AND KEEPING THE BEST EMPLOYEES

Books by Robert Half

The Robert Half Way to Get Hired in Today's Job Market
Robert Half's Success Guide for Accountants
Robert Half on Hiring
Making It Big in Data Processing
How to Get a Better Job in This Crazy World
Finding, Hiring, and Keeping the Best Employees

FINDING, HIRING, AND KEEPING THE BEST EMPLOYEES

ROBERT HALF

WILEY

John Wiley & Sons, Inc.

New York • Chichester • Brisbane • Toronto • Singapore

Copyright © 1993 by Robert Half International, Inc.
Published by John Wiley & Sons, Inc.

Library of Congress Cataloging-in-Publication Data:
Half, Robert.
    Finding, hiring, and keeping the best employees / Robert Half.
      p.   cm.
    Includes index.
    ISBN 0-471-58510-6 (alk. paper)
    1. Employee selection.   2. Compensation management.   I. Title.
    HF5549.5.S38H34   1993
    658.3'11—dc20   93-19574

Printed in the United States of America

10 9 8 7 6 5 4 3

"Life is the ultimate revolving door."

In memory of my friends:

Robert S. Boas
Charles J. Cole
Leonard Ugelow
Milton Weinick

CONTENTS

ACKNOWLEDGMENTS

It takes more than one to get things done

Robert Half International, Inc. has continually supported educational projects to supply helpful information to the workplace. This book is one. I want to thank my friend Harold M. Messmer, Jr., Chairman and CEO of the company, for his encouragement.

Lynn Taylor, Vice President of Corporate Communications, along with Steve Pehanich and Annette Mowinckle were of great help with research. Don Bain, Laurie Wilson, and Ruth Lazzara were there for editorial advice, along with Ruth Mills of John Wiley & Sons.

Patrick Griffin, someone I could always bank on, pitched in when necessary.

INTRODUCTION

"A revolving door turns both ways."

Someone once defined *frustration* as trying to slam a revolving door. In the business world, the challenge of hiring and retaining good people can not only be frustrating, the ramifications of failure can be serious at best.

Companies with revolving doors, through which the best and brightest come and go, function at a disadvantage. No company, large or small, is defined by board rooms, products, services, marketing plans, corporate logos, and other tangible manifestations of "doing business." They are defined by *people*. In racetrack parlance it can be put, "Bet on the jockey, not on the horse."

These are trying times for employers looking to identify, hire, and retain good people. Because of a variety of factors, the pool of educated, experienced, and otherwise qualified job candidates is less deep, and it promises to become even more shallow in years ahead. This means, of course, that those men and women in the labor force who possess requisite skills and knowledge are increasingly at a premium. Competition for their services will certainly heat up.

THE EDUCATION PROBLEM

Although the figures change depending upon who presents them, there is some support to the thesis that the United States has, and will continue to have, less qualified people to carry its business banner through the 1990s and beyond.

Statistics developed by the Southport Institute for Policy Analysis, a Washington, D.C.–based research organization, represent the consensus. Southport estimated at the end of 1989 that between 20 and 30 million adult Americans had serious problems at work and in their everyday lives due to insufficient basic skills.

1

Other studies are equally as sobering:

- On a scale of one to six (with six being the highest), the average American 20- to 25-year-old reads at a level of 2.6, according to a study conducted at the end of the previous decade by the U.S. Department of Labor. Current jobs demand a minimum reading level of 3.0. By the year 2000, new jobs will require that level to be raised to 3.6 in order for workers to understand basic instruction manuals and company directives.

- Despite an increasing need for science-trained men and women to function in high-tech jobs that demand such a background, the National Academy of Sciences cautioned in 1990 that there might well be a shortfall of 400,000 science graduates by the year 2000.

- In May, 1990, the Commission on the Skills of the American Workforce, established by the nonprofit National Center on Education and the Economy, compared the United States with a number of foreign countries as to how they train high school graduates for the job market. The United States ranked near the bottom.

- Many of these individuals do not, and will not, possess the basic reading, writing, and math skills necessary to maintain a company's competitive position, much less help it to grow.

- According to the U.S. Labor Department, most of America's uneducated workers will be from minority groups, and will fill 56 percent of new jobs developed in the 1990s.

- A recent *Wall Street Journal* article reported that a survey of Fortune 500 companies indicated that 58 percent complained of having trouble finding employees with basic skills.

- The National Association of Temporary Services projects an eventual need for the United States to import as many as one million skilled workers to substitute for American workers lacking those skills.

Yet, in the face of these and hundreds of equally telling studies, too many American firms continue to be shortsighted in their attempt to downsize. Economist Richard F. Hokenson of Donaldson, Lufkin & Jenrette Securities Corporation points to a trend by American business to encourage trained and experienced male workers in the 45 to 54 age bracket to leave the workforce. In doing so, he cautions, U.S. corporations "are throwing away their seed corn at the very time that labor shortages loom ahead."

THE TRAINING PROBLEM

Worker trainer by industry will loom large. Companies will not only have to hire the best talent available, but they will also have to institute programs to upgrade skills, improve knowledge, and motivate enhanced performance. Are companies prepared to do this?

According to a 1990 study conducted by the Commission on the Skills of the American Workforce, less than 30 percent of companies say they are willing to incorporate special programs for women, immigrants, and minority youth; only 15 percent worry about shortages of skilled workers; more than 80 percent shun basic skills in favor of a worker's attitude and personality.

PEOPLE ARE YOUR MOST IMPORTANT ASSET

Companies that establish an enlightened policy of "hiring smart," retaining, and training will have more than a leg-up on their competition. They will be poised to flourish in the difficult years ahead because their *people* will be the best, will stay and grow with them, and will demonstrate a brand of loyalty that is vital to long-term success.

People!

An enterprising computer manufacturer only happens to make computers. More accurately, it is a group of people functioning together for a common purpose—making and selling computer equipment.

A bank is known for the services it provides. But those services are nothing more than ideas conceived and executed by the people who created them.

The people who are hired to advance a business' interests will determine whether it succeeds or fails. If a company does happen to find the right people—and they leave to work for its competitors—much has been lost.

Richard S. Sloma, author of *The Turnaround Manager's Handbook* (New York: Collier MacMillan, 1985), wrote, "People are a firm's most important asset. If you have an excellent product but only mediocre people, the results will be only mediocre." In the words of a sage out of the Yogi Berra–Casey Stengel school, "Good people do good work; lousy people don't."

There is nothing profound or new in advocating the hiring of good people. It's axiomatic. It's basic. It's smart. Why then do so many otherwise savvy companies fail to do just that—to "hire smart?" Why do so many otherwise astute companies lose too many of the good people they managed to hire in the first place?

That's what this book is about, the hiring and retention of quality men and women to stand watch over our business interests in the turbulent, challenging decades ahead. It could be called the "finders-keepers" approach to staffing. Companies good at it are more likely to succeed. Companies that fail to find and keep the best employees may well end up "losers-weepers."

The widespread layoffs of the recent recession certainly contribute to the employee revolving door addressed by this book. Our economy runs in cycles. We prosper, grow, hire, and fatten our employee rosters. Then, the economy takes a downturn and we cull and slenderize. We dismiss people, tighten our belts, and make do with fewer people who are asked to do more. Inevitable? Hardly.

The overall staffing strategy of any company can avoid being overly sensitive to outside forces. If a company has analyzed staffing needs carefully, has hired smart, and has put into action the sort of motivational and career-inspiring programs needed to retain the best people, it need not ride the ebb and flow of the national economy, at least not where it involves its employees.

SMART HIRING

The Labor Department estimated that as of 1992 the average cost of hiring just one worker is $40,000. Employee turnover can be deadly to a company, both in cost and morale. Yet, thanks to smart hiring techniques, costly turnovers can be minimized.

Hiring smart takes commitment to a carefully conceived and constructed hiring and retention philosophy and program. Over the years there has been a tendency on the part of too many companies to view the hiring process as something that "just gets done." Busy managers, anxious to fill a slot and get on with it, hire accordingly. They fill an opening with what they consider to be the best person available after going through a cursory selection process. They hire on intuition, by the seat of their pants. They assume the resumes they've read accurately reflect the candidates. Check references? Who has time for that? Maybe a phone call or two.

Some companies hire on the theory that if new people don't work out, there's always the revolving door through which to send them. Others scrutinize resumes, choose the person with the best paper credentials, and conduct the interview as a necessary evil, a few general questions interrupted by phone calls and visitors.

Of course, there are many companies considerably more dedicated to finding and hiring the right people. They take great pains to determine those candidates who define work as a four-letter word to which they're allergic, and those who view work as a four-letter word that spells loyalty, commitment, productivity, achievement, and success.

NURTURING AND MOTIVATING

Some companies, after successfully weeding out the good from the bad, fail to realize (or to act on the realization) that the process of finders-keepers has only been half fulfilled. Unless the "right person" is nurtured from his or her first day on the job, chances are good that the company's revolving door will be sought by that individual, perhaps to provide skill and knowledge to a competitor.

Because the companies of the future will, of necessity, be forced to accomplish more with fewer people, the quality of those people is paramount. At the same time, once they've been chosen and begin work, they will have established themselves as prime commodities in the hiring marketplace. Whether they decide to stay with their current employers or to seek free-agency, will be determined by how they're treated, and the opportunities open to them.

Like the hiring process itself, motivation of employees doesn't just happen. It must come out of a concerted and ongoing effort to create, and put into action, new and innovative ways to inspire the best in every employee, at every level. As IBM's Thomas J. Watson, Jr., put it, "I believe the real difference between success and failure in a corporation can very often be traced to the question of how well the organization brings out the great energies and talents of its people."

Finding, hiring, and retaining the best people *can be taught*. Time-honored principles are there to be emulated and integrated into a company's overall approach to staffing and motivating. At the same time, new and creative ideas must be sought out and melded with proven approaches.

The idea of choosing an employee of the month has been around for a long time, but a textile company in St. Louis took the concept a step further. A parking spot next to the president's is reserved for the chosen employee, and his or her name is displayed there. It is an old idea made better by someone committed to employee motivation.

It is the intention of *Finding, Hiring, and Keeping the Best Employees* to encourage large and small companies to focus new energy and attention on the critical function of hiring and retaining top-notch employees. The ideas and concepts presented in this book work. The benefits gained by those who have put them into practice are considerable.

If you and your company enjoy some of those same benefits after reading this book, the efforts of writing it will have been more than justified.

Robert Half

PART I

FINDING AND HIRING THE RIGHT EMPLOYEES

1

ETHICS FIRST

Creating an Ethical Company

"If you think it might not be ethical—it isn't."

After a decade of distinctly unethical behavior in segments of the business world, *ethics* has become a popular buzzword. The reality of the recent recession has sent companies scurrying in search of more back-to-basics thinking. They hear and read of the need to rediscover old-fashioned values—surely redefined by new-fashioned pressures, but encompassing such staples as honor, courage, commitment, and, yes, ethics. It's okay to be ethical again.

Because this swing of the pendulum affects every facet of our lives, its impact upon how business is conducted in the years ahead will be profound. Sure, it is good to behave ethically and fairly in personal dealings, but it's also *good business* whether or not it's currently fashionable.

There's nothing mysterious or altruistic when a company commits to ethical behavior. Companies that stand behind their products and services, that advertise responsibly, and that conduct day-to-day activities in an aboveboard and legal manner are respected by their customers. They nurture brand loyalty, and enjoy the fruits of repeat business.

We've all had the experience of being given a quote of, say, $500 to make unnecessary repairs on an automobile or appliance, and then receiving another quote to fix the real problem for a fraction of that amount. Guess which repair person we go to in the future.

While a company's reputation for ethical dealings is scrutinized by its customers, it is also judged by another important constituency—

potential employees. If a company wants to hire ethical people (and I assume that most do), but has failed to establish itself as an ethical company, the task is difficult. Word gets around. For the most qualified and appealing job candidates whose services are in demand, their choice will be simple. They will choose to work where their own ethical standards are more closely matched to that of their employer.

Companies that have failed to establish a strong sense of corporate ethics will, of course, always find people to hire—but at a premium price. To attract good people, these companies must pay more than companies that are not perceived as being ethical. Their revolving doors usually turn faster than their more ethical competitors.

CREATE AN ETHICAL COMPANY

The first step of finding and keeping good people is to create a first-class organization in every sense of the word. This involves creating

- A safe and pleasant work environment
- A system of compensation and advancement potential that is fair and equitable
- Challenging work
- Astute and inspiring management
- A business reputation that allows employees to believe in what they do and to hold their heads high with family and friends

Like the hiring process itself, though, ethics is too often *assumed*. Upper levels of management might be staffed with ethical and decent people, but that doesn't mean the *company* can be assumed to follow suit. In many cases it will. In others, the assumption won't match reality. Robert Noyce, an inventor of the silicon chip, once put it, "I don't believe unethical people get ahead in business. If ethics are poor at the top, that behavior is copied down through the organization."

CAN ETHICS BE TAUGHT?

Judging from the number of courses being offered in colleges and universities and by major corporations, the attitude of those spearheading these efforts seem to be that ethics can be taught. If nothing else, such training establishes a set of guidelines. The fewer gray areas the better, where ethics is concerned.

Others argue that adult employees cannot be educated to behave ethically. Either they bring to the workplace a sense of ethics, or they don't. As Paul Towne, corporate director of ethics at Honeywell, once said, the company expects employees to "bring their ethics to work with them." At the same time, Honeywell has always placed emphasis on hiring employees whose ethical standards meet the company's lofty expectations. When hiring is done with that in mind, corporate training on ethical behavior becomes less necessary, except for defining specific company guidelines.

An even better approach combines the two philosophies. Hire ethical people and reinforce their ethical behavior by setting policy and demanding strict adherence to it.

A 1990 article in the *Harvard Business Review*, written by Kenneth Andrews, stated, "No matter how much colleges and business schools expand their investment in moral instruction, most education in business ethics (as in all other aspects of business acumen) will occur in the organizations in which people spend their lives. . . . Policy is implicit in behavior."

ADVERTISE YOUR COMPANY'S ETHICAL STANDARDS

Assume that both management and a company's daily operations are ethical. Is that sufficient when seeking to hire and retain the sort of employees needed to carry the company's business into the competitive future? Perhaps not. A company must *communicate* its commitment to ethics to the shrinking pool of the best educated and most capable candidates if they are to be aware of it.

The lowering of ethical standards in business during the high-flying '80s has left a skeptical taste in many mouths: "All business is unethical." Those possessing that attitude might view an ethical company with the same jaded, broad-brush outlook. An upstanding, ethical company runs the risk of losing these people as employees because it didn't bother to communicate to them its ethical commitment. The great showman, P.T. Barnum, once defined public relations as, "Do good, and tell about it."

It is my belief, based on more than 45 years in matching the right people to the right jobs, that not only must ethical behavior be raised to a new level of priority in American companies, but a simultaneous thrust must also be triggered to "tell about it." Before an advertisement announcing a new job opening is ever placed, the prevailing "belief" in the business world at-large should be that this is an honest, ethical, good place to work. Establish that in the public mind and a larger pool of quality job candidates will seek to fill that job.

Robert Half International's corporate motto is "Ethics First." It doesn't represent lip-service; we believe in it.

At the time our company was first established, there were some individuals whose unethical dealings gave the entire personnel service industry a bad name. Our commitment to ethics, therefore, was decidedly self-serving. Because we gradually became known for our Ethics First approach, our business grew.

At the same time, the people we attracted as employees represented the best available, and continue to do so. Simply put, add a solid reputation for ethical behavior to a competitive salary and benefits package, and bright, talented, and committed people will be attracted.

The advantages of attracting and hiring ethical employees are numerous—and obvious. Employee theft is the most definitive example. Employee theft is estimated to cost American businesses $120 billion annually, according to studies by the *Journal of Accountancy*. This accounts for "hard theft," the taking of tangible materials.

Here are other advantages of hiring ethical employees:

- Ethical employees don't steal an employer's time or materials.
- Ethical employees don't reveal trade secrets to competitors.
- Ethical employees don't use their employer's resources and time to pursue personal and/or other business interests.
- Ethical employees stay in their jobs longer.
- Ethical employees don't resign without giving fair notice.

For employees, working for an ethical company reaps similar rewards. The ethical company

- Treats employees fairly
- Respects employees as people
- Provides growth opportunities within the company, thus lessening the need for employees to look elsewhere for career advancement
- Doesn't ask employees to do anything illegal, immoral, or unethical

- Enables employees to speak with pride to their communities about what they do for a living, and for whom they do it

As with any business entity, the ethical climate is established at the top and trickles down to every level. Unethical management sends a message to its employees that it's okay to function on a lower ethical plane. Management that pressures employees to compromise personal ethics to achieve corporate goals do these individuals a disservice.

HIRE ETHICAL EMPLOYEES

Will ethical companies always manage to land the best job candidates? In a perfect world, they would, but perfection is, as we all know, impossible to achieve. What is important is that if companies seeking to find, hire, and retain the best employees blend a strong and public commitment to ethics into their hiring process, their chances for success are enhanced.

The positive image of industries and professions also plays an important role in generating a larger pool of quality job applicants. It behooves every company, along with the industry associations to which it belongs, to set higher ethical standards and to communicate this to the public at-large. Again, it not only is good for business, it creates a hiring climate more conducive to attracting better employees to its ranks.

Is there a generation gap where ethics are concerned? Up-and-coming young managers in the '80s, particularly in the financial services industry, were often viewed as lacking in ethical principles. Certain surveys substantiate that perception. A study conducted in the early '80s by the Gallup organization, in conjunction with the *Wall Street Journal*, indicated that younger Americans were more likely to take unethical paths than were their older counterparts. While only 26 percent of the respondents over the age of 50 admitted to taking home work supplies, 50 percent in their thirties and forties confessed to the practice. The same study indicated that only 18 percent of those over 50 admitted to have called in falsely sick, while 40 percent under 40 admitted to having done so. Among executives, 41 percent under the age of 50 said they'd overstated their income tax deductions, whereas 24 percent of the older group said they had.

While interesting, such surveys have little practical use when it comes to making hiring decisions. In the first place, to choose a candidate for a position based upon age is blatantly illegal. In the second place, this information hampers hiring authorities rather than aids them. Bringing preconceived prejudices to the hiring process arbitrarily limits the field of good candidates, and is unethical.

Ethics, I believe, belongs to no generation, gender, nor ethnic, religious or national origin. It is an individual matter, nurtured certainly by society and prevailing business mores, but hardly predicated by any study, survey, or popular myth. Making a hiring decision based upon such factors is not only unethical, it's also bad business.

Is it possible to accurately judge a potential employee's ethical fiber before the job is offered? To a certain extent, I believe it is, and every effort should be made to do so.

A company's entire reputation can be tainted by the misdeeds of *one* individual. Although there is no fool-proof way to anticipate any individual's actions at a given point—and under specific pressures—management has an obligation to do everything possible to hire the caliber of people who are *unlikely* to act in a way that would impact negatively on the company. Specific suggestions on how to accomplish this appear in subsequent chapters on evaluating resumes, conducting interviews, and checking references.

The first and most important step, however, is a *commitment* to hiring ethical people. It should be as firm a commitment as seeking out people with the requisite background, skills, and experience to do the job. Candidates seeking to fill a position should be made aware at the first contact that the company believes in and operates from a solid ethical foundation, and expects every employee to follow suit. This isn't a statement of moral belief. It should be a statement of conviction that a company committed to doing business ethically is a better, more successful company, and certainly a better place to work.

2

"MIRROR, MIRROR ON THE WALL . . ."

Improving the Corporate Image

"It's not only what we are that counts, it's what people think we are."

Communicating a company's ethical commitment to a shrinking field of qualified job candidates is, of course, a public relations (PR) function. In PR parlance, we're talking about projecting the proverbial corporate image.

A corporation's image, at times and under certain circumstances, can be misleading. Sometimes this is done deliberately. However, because we've become more sophisticated in our ability to judge "images" created by skilled public relations professionals, we are better able to see through attempts to project an image that hasn't been earned. That's why I prefer the word *reflection* instead of the word *image*.

The great showman, P.T. Barnum, once described public relations as, "Do good and tell about it"—two distinctly different parts of the public relations equation. There are many elements of a company's reflection in addition to whether it holds itself to a high ethical standard. Some are tangible and visible; others are more subtle. In either case—and including ethics—they encompass the "do good" aspect of Barnum's definition. A company must create a compelling corporate reflection through deeds, rather than words; otherwise, job candidates, who are in demand by many companies, will see a less desirable corporate mirror-image. All the "telling about it" won't effectively mask the reality.

LOOK FOR SOCIALLY RESPONSIBLE EMPLOYEES

Many of today's young people, while as career-driven as their counterparts from previous generations, carry additional commitments to a variety of causes that did not play a significant role in years past. As the ethical pendulum makes its slow but steady swing back to a more reasoned center, a parallel growth of "life values" has emerged.

Job candidates with strong environmental concerns may add them to the list of considerations when choosing between job offers. Given a relatively equitable package of salary, benefits, and potentials for career growth, a company with a strong and public track record of concern for the environment will often tip the scales in its favor. A 1991 Maritz Telephone Survey, in *Quick Marketing Magazine*, discovered that 86 percent of *all* Americans felt that a company's environmental reputation was important. Similarly, job candidates with all the right professional credentials, but who also actively participate in projects to aid the homeless, will view positively a company that has demonstrated active concern for community affairs, and that has turned such concern into action.

ESTABLISH A POSITIVE CORPORATE REPUTATION

The global nature of business has taken center-stage. Competition from the Pacific Rim, and now the burgeoning industrial clout of a unified European Community, has encouraged career-minded American men and women to look abroad for additional opportunities. Given a choice between a company whose eyes are, at least, open to growth potential in other nations, and one that proudly wears industrial isolationist blinders, there is little doubt which will attract this breed of candidate.

To what extent is a company committed to personal and professional growth of its employees through company-sponsored programs of continuing education? Are its employees enrolled in local colleges and universities, enhancing their knowledge and skills with the company's support? If so, both employee and company ultimately benefit. These same employees will be "telling about it" in a more effective way than any company press release could accomplish. They constitute a vitally important arm of "corporate networking," a recruit-ing tool that has become increasingly important in these days of competition for the best and the brightest. (Recruiting is discussed more extensively in Chapter 7.)

How does a company treat its suppliers and competitors? Is it known by its suppliers as a responsible customer, or one that poses an ongoing headache for the accounts-payable department? When com-peting with other companies in its field, does it function aboveboard and honestly, or has it gained the negative reputation of applying unethical, perhaps even illegal, tactics?

A firm that respects and values the contributions of working par-ents, employees of diverse ethnic, religious, and national origins, and those with "handicaps" will attract the best of them. In addition, these employees won't hesitate to tell others that "it's a great place to work."

A COMPELLING CORPORATE REFLECTION HELPS THE RECRUITING PROCESS

The purpose of this book is not to preach to any company on how to conduct business, but when it comes to the difference between sterling candidates accepting a job offer or the company's choosing to forfeit talents to a competitor, the importance of a positive corporate reflec-tion cannot be denied.

Companies that have established themselves positively in the pub-lic eye are natural magnets for good people. We are all aware of such companies. They've routinely "done good" as part of their basic busi-ness philosophy, and have communicated these values to the world at-large.

Quality has nothing to do with size, geographic location, product or services offered, or industry served. Quality companies come in all sizes, shapes, and corporate cultures. A small, dynamic software firm in Silicon Valley, with a relaxed culture and team approach, will naturally attract employees who respond favorably to that atmosphere. Other large companies, with a more structured approach, will be palatable for others.

Despite a conducive atmosphere, however, if a company's general reputation—its reflection—is less than positive, there will be problems recruiting good employees, unless, of course, the company is forced to pay more to acquire them.

Companies with solid reputations for ethics, community service, and environmental concerns have spent money to achieve that positive corporate reflection. If they had not spent money to enhance the way they're perceived by the public—including potential employees—would the savings make up for higher salaries needed to attract the right people? Perhaps, but only from a short-term perspective. Over the long term, it will have been money well invested. Companies that want to succeed will reap continuing benefits through the hiring and retention of good people.

It isn't surprising that many companies are unaware of their corporate reflections, positive or negative. The reason is usually that they haven't taken stock, haven't held up a thermometer to public perception. In some instances, companies really don't want to know. The truth would be too painful. In most cases, however, they simply haven't thought to do it. It isn't difficult to determine one's corporate reflection, provided it's done openly and honestly and avoids the route taken by politicians who commission polls calculated to tell them all is well, especially when it isn't.

For companies whose staffing practices have always been to seek out, hire, and nurture good, honest, ethical employees, the sort of positive corporate reflection necessary to attract other quality people will already have been established. For companies that agree with the message of this book, but who have not, as yet, paid sufficient attention to their corporate reflection, it's time to start. In either case, employees who represent a company—who create its products and services and market them to the consumer, who *are* the company—hold the key. If the right people have been hired, their values will become those of the company. *They* will be the corporate reflection that attracts others of similar attributes and values.

At Robert Half International, we have interviewed numerous, quality job candidates who, when told there's an opening at a specific company, have said, "I've always wanted to work there." We have also heard candidates respond with, "I hear a lot of bad things about that company." The difference is clear when it comes to hiring and retaining good people. Excellent job candidates are selective and insist on working with companies that enjoy a good reputation.

3

LEGAL EAGLES

Avoiding Employment Lawsuits

"To sue or not to sue is no longer the question."

It wasn't long ago that employment-related lawsuits were relatively rare. The courts tended to side with employers when such cases were litigated; even when the ruling was in favor of the plaintiff (employee), damages were small, usually covering only the amount of wages actually lost. As a result, attorneys were reluctant to take on such cases, especially on a contingency basis.

That scenario changed, however. Personal injury lawyers, accustomed to enjoying large jury awards for clients who had suffered pain and suffering because of someone else's negligence, became aggressive in skirting legal formalities and bringing employment suits to sympathetic juries as quickly as possible. Dismissed employees or those claiming they were not offered a job because of discrimination were increasingly compensated for the pain and suffering inflicted on them by unfair employer conduct.

The impact of this type of litigation has been dramatic. In the '90s, there are more employment-related lawsuits being filed than personal injury suits. Jury awards in employment cases are routinely into six figures and employees are winning many more cases. As a result of this groundswell of civil litigation in matters of employment, a rich file of legal precedents upon which to support attorneys' arguments has mushroomed.

That the United States has become the most litigious society in the world is beyond debate. Former Chrysler chairman Lee Iacocca is fond of telling the story of a tree that grew in the middle of the Sahara Desert: There was no other vegetation within hundreds of miles. During World War II, a British tank driver ran into the tree. Iacocca finishes the story by adding, "If it happened today in this country, he'd sue. I don't know who he'd sue, but he'd sue."

This penchant to sue touches every aspect of our lives; its ramifications for American business are especially damaging—and confusing. Problematic employees whose employment could once be terminated at management's discretion through "good cause" now turn to the courts for redress, and often win.

EMPLOYERS' LIABILITY IS INCREASING

Today's employer has more to worry about than being accused of an unfair dismissal of a troublesome employee, or failing to hire someone because of perceived prejudice in the decision. As expected, the liability of employers for their employees' conduct now extends beyond the workplace. Consider these examples:

- A Texas cab company was sued for $5 million after one of its drivers raped a passenger. The plaintiff won.

- A security guard at a Miami bank killed a fellow guard, and was judged mentally incompetent to stand trial. The slain guard's widow sued the bank for failure to have adequately researched the murderer's history of mental stability. The bank settled.

- A guard for a major national security company stole a large sum of money from one of the firm's Rhode Island clients. The security firm had thoroughly checked the guard's references, including a search for prior criminal convictions. No criminal history was found, and every reference had positive things to say about the guard. Still, the client sued, the jury found in its favor, and the Rhode Island Supreme Court ruled that where "sensitive" jobs are involved, an employer must adequately research a potential employee's past, even when initial queries fail to turn up negative information.

There are thousands of such lawsuits each year, and they touch on every facet of the relationship between employer and employee, employer and prospective employee, and even employer and past employees. Employer liability is not necessarily limited to employee misconduct while on the job, a situation covered under the legal concept of *respondeat superior.* Employers have been held liable for injuries caused by the employee *outside* the employment arena. Never before has there been such a critical need to evaluate a prospective employee thoroughly before offering the job. Checking references is a key factor and is examined in-depth in Chapter 13.

Wrongful discharge is another area of litigation that today's employers must face. Jury Verdict Research Inc., based in Solon, Ohio, is a private organization that monitors jury decisions throughout the country. It reports that a former employee who sues a private company for wrongful discharge has an 86 percent chance of winning the case, as opposed to a 33 percent chance for a similar suit against a government-run business (*Nation's Business*; July 1989).

Every aspect of the employer-employee relationship has been impacted. The legal ramifications of hiring, retaining, promoting, compensating, interviewing, reference-checking, and firing are considerable. In general, however, companies wishing to minimize the risk of becoming embroiled in employer-employee litigation must begin by acknowledging the possibility of its happening, no matter how well intentioned management might be. Just as the hiring process cannot be left to chance and intuition, the reality of today's legal climate cannot be ignored.

REVIEW YOUR EMPLOYMENT PRACTICES TO AVOID LEGAL PROBLEMS

Enlightened companies are building an annual legal checkup into their budgets. It's money well spent. Should you decide to do so, have an attorney knowledgeable in the field of employment law review such areas as

- Employee handbooks
- Employment applications
- Hiring practices
- Firing policies
- Rules of employee conduct
- Workplace safety and security
- Performance reviews
- Salary increases and promotions

A legal review can head off future legal problems.

Recently, some employers have been building into conditions of employment a contract that contains a provision precluding disgruntled ex-employees from taking civil action, and limiting them to arbitration. The U.S. Supreme Court has ruled in one case that a 62-year-old worker could not sue a former employer for age discrimination because he had signed such a contract when taking the job. The court rejected the notion that his right to bring action in civil court had been guaranteed by the Age Discrimination in Employment Act.

KEEP IN MIND LEGAL ISSUES WHEN INTERVIEWING JOB CANDIDATES

It's not only lawyers who should be involved in evaluating and implementing a company's employment policies. If the company's commitment to ethical, legal employment practices is part-and-parcel of its business philosophy, the company must ensure that every employee in a responsible position be aware of the pitfalls into which they might step, even inadvertently. A careless comment to a job candidate by a company employee, who has not benefitted from at least a cursory education in the company's employment practices, could become the basis for future legal action. Promising job candidates that they will be secure in their job at the company, will never be fired unless they deserve to be, or that the position they're interviewing for is a permanent one, could cause employment-related legal actions. Ten years ago, such comments were considered innocuous. Today, they can land companies in court.

Discrimination based on age, gender, religion, and national origin is a common area of offense. While presumably everyone knows that it is blatantly illegal to discriminate in hiring based on these factors, there is an increasing number of subtle mistakes an employer can make that may lead to legal action. Requesting that a candidate's photograph accompany an employment application, asking for his or her place of birth, and inquiring into a woman's plans for starting a family have all been considered to be in violation of today's employment law. Privacy in the workplace has also become a popular legal issue as more companies test employees for drug and alcohol abuse and utilize electronic technology to monitor performance.

These issues contribute to a legal minefield for even the most well-intentioned company and management to traverse. No book, including this one, can or should attempt to offer legal advice. However, if there is one thing a book on hiring, retaining, and firing should attempt to do, it is to raise the awareness of American companies concerning the integral relationship between staffing a company effectively and the legal ramifications of failing to do so lawfully and ethically. It has been said that "nice" doctors are rarely sued for malpractice. The same thesis applies to nice companies. Many employee law suits may be sparked by vindictiveness, but when there is a healthy company spirit, employees are less likely to sue, and are even discouraged from doing so by contented colleagues.

4

THE FOLLY OF DISCRIMINATION IN THE WORKPLACE

Preventing Discriminatory Hiring Practices

"Bias in employment is a crime against humanity."

Discrimination in the workplace is illegal and immoral. It's also bad business. For example, suppose an employer decides that a job should be filled by a man, preferably of the same race and national origin as others in the department and between the ages of 35 and 45. Because it is illegal to advertise these requisites, the ad indicates that the job is open to all: "We are an equal opportunity employer." Most of the time that's true, but all too often it's a perfunctory phrase thrown in for legal reasons.

DON'T LIMIT THE POOL OF APPLICANTS

Although some companies run the risk of legal sanctions—and rightly so—that isn't the thrust of this book. From its perspective, companies that place these and other artificial restrictions on hiring only end up severely limiting their ability to choose from the richest possible talent pool.

Naturally, there are jobs that demand certain abilities that rule out selected people. A physically demanding job might necessitate hiring workers who are stronger than others. This sort of situation constitutes only a small percentage of hiring decisions, however. In most cases, a wide range of individuals is capable of filling a position—men or women, young or old, people of every race, religion, or national origin. Given that candidates from each group possess comparable education, knowledge, and skills—in other words, have the skills to get the job done—why limit the choice to only those who meet arbitrary, biased, preconceived notions?

As pointed out in the Introduction, the United States is faced with a dwindling number of qualified workers. Minorities and women will increasingly represent the available talent and will occupy a majority of jobs in the future. Does artificially limiting the scope of a hiring search make sense in that climate? Of course not. Purchasing agents routinely survey the field of suppliers in search of the best product, at the best price. They invite bids from all who can deliver what the company needs. Human resources professionals, and the management for whom they hire, should do no less.

DON'T PRE-JUDGE JOB CANDIDATES

Aside from the obvious forms of employment prejudice—gender, age, race, religion—there are many other subtle, albeit telling, pre-judgments that limit the field of candidates from which to choose. Here are three to watch out for:

- Don't choose a candidate on the basis of appearance or personality. "If they look like us, dress like us, speak like us, and think like us, they must be okay." Not necessarily.
- Don't rely on test scores. "Only those who score above a certain level will be considered." Remember that tests don't necessarily measure "smarts" or people skills or the ability to be a team player. Medical schools, for example, are filled with students whose grades were at the top. Whether they have the other less tangible qualities necessary to become caring, healing physicians remains conjecture. Being an effective employee in any field or profession demands more than just qualitative knowledge.

  Employment testing (discussed in detail in Chapter 12) can play a role in the ultimate hiring decision, but it shouldn't be the only determining factor.

- Beware of school prejudice. One of the most common hiring prejudices is to choose only from those employees who've graduated from a select list of colleges and universities. A certain amount of this might result from campus recruiting efforts, but to follow it as a hiring philosophy is to lose sight of the obvious. If you examine the educational background of some of the world's most successful business people, you will find that only a small percentage graduated from prestigious schools. Impressive sheepskins do not necessarily translate into quality employees. Educational quality is important, but even more meaningful is what a person is made of: character, drive, willingness to learn and to grow, honesty, and the commitment to a company's goals and philosophies.

HOW TO BROADEN THE POOL OF INTERVIEWEES

Total objectivity in hiring is impossible to achieve, especially when more than one person is involved in the selection process. Assume you will be the supervisor of a candidate who is yet to be hired. One hundred fifty resumes have been received by the human resources department, which sorts them into three piles: likely candidates; good candidates, but not as good as the first batch; and those who lack the requisite skills and experience for the job.

The sorting of candidates is done, of course, by people to whom the chosen candidate will *not* report. For that reasons, it would behoove you to interview not only, say, five from the first pile, but also a few from the runner-up stack, even if you pick them at random. Chances are good that at least one from the "not-as-good" pile will, in your estimation, compare favorably with the five primary candidates.

It may seem axiomatic, but one of the best ways to eliminate silent prejudices is to pay careful attention to *those who do the hiring*. It's akin to choosing a jury. Stock a human resources department with "jurors" who are relatively free of bias, and you stand the best chance of finding, hiring, and retaining the best available candidates.

HOW DISCRIMINATION LAWS AFFECT EMPLOYMENT PRACTICES

Federal groundwork against workplace discrimination was established in 1964 when Title VII of the Civil Rights Act was enacted. It prohibited companies from bias in hiring, promoting, or dismissing, or in pay and benefits, on the basis of race, color, religion, gender, or national origin.

The terms of that Act have been broadened to include persons over the age of 40, disabled veterans, Vietnam-era veterans, and the handicapped. In 1978, Congress amended the law to include the Pregnancy Discrimination Act, which covered pregnancy, childbirth, and related medical problems. More recently, the Supreme Court ruled to include sexual harassment.

As the 1990s dawned, AIDS and other transmittable diseases have become the basis for discrimination lawsuits. Alcoholics and drug addicts have also sought and found protection under the statutes.

Employment law evolves from a complex, crazy-quilt mix of Federal and state legislation. No book can or should attempt to replace the advice of a company's legal counsel, but from a general hiring-and-firing perspective, there are basic legal tenets to which all employers must adhere, regardless of the jurisdiction under which they do business.

Firing

First, understand that it *is* legal to fire an employee, but be prepared to document the reasons for termination. For example, the following lists some acceptable reasons:

- Substandard performance
- Excessive absenteeism or lateness
- Lack of ethics
- Failure to obey laws affecting the business
- Embezzlement
- Disruptive behavior

It is unlawful to fire employees if their only offense was to exercise legal rights. According to Michael Lotito, a labor law specialist at the firm of Jackson, Lewis, Schnitzler & Krupman, such legal rights include

- Asking for time to serve on a jury
- Filing a workers compensation claim, or a complaint with the state wage-and-hour board
- Refusing to commit an impropriety, such as falsifying documentation that will be submitted to a court or regulatory agency

Of course, it is also illegal to fire any individual for other than work-related reasons. Chapter 28 discusses the unpleasant (albeit often necessary) task of dismissing an employee. Suffice it to say at this time that unless an employee's performance not only is deemed sub-par but also has been thoroughly documented as such, the legal arena is where any dispute is likely to be settled.

Sexual Discrimination and Harassment

Sexual harassment is one of the most heated areas of employment discrimination, and is among the most difficult for employees to prove. (The Clarence Thomas Supreme Court confirmation hearings, if nothing else, pointed out the many difficulties inherent in the investigation of sexual harassment charges.) An allegation of wrongdoing, whether or not ultimately proved, can severely damage a company's reputation as an employer, to say nothing of the time and money needed to defend against such charges.

An increasing number of companies have instituted educational programs through which employees learn what constitutes sexual harassment, and how to avoid behavior that might be construed as harassment. Most important, management must take a stand—be on the record as neither condoning nor allowing any form of sexual harassment, and act against those who violate that principle.

Age Discrimination

The number of legal actions brought against employers for hiring discrimination based on age has grown dramatically in recent years; damages awarded have kept pace with the increase in actions filed. A 1989 study published by the Bureau of National Affairs, a private Washington-based information service, pegs the average age discrimination award at $722,294, which doesn't take into account, of course, the money spent by a company to defend itself.

To return to the prevailing theme of this book, though, age discrimination can be costly in other ways. In the days ahead, older workers will become increasingly in demand and valued. Demographic projections in the U.S. Census Bureau indicate that by the year 2000, the population will increase 7.1 percent. Unlike previous population swells, however, this will result from people living longer, rather than because of higher birth rates, and will have a serious impact on the availability of workers between the ages of 30 and 45.

Older employees can be an asset to any company. Ironically, it is often older job candidates themselves who add to their difficulty in being hired. I have found that they enter an interview *assuming* they will be discriminated against. Rather than demonstrate all the positive reasons why they are right for the job, they act defensively. (The same, of course, holds true for all categories of job seekers who establish a negative, defensive posture rather than putting forward their best positive foot). Once such a barrier has been erected, it often becomes self-fulfilling.

An interviewer can do a great deal, however, to overcome this in the interest of fairly evaluating an older candidate's qualifications. The first step is to be free of prejudices toward older workers in general and to recognize that older employees are often more ethical on the job and bring years of experience to a company that cannot easily be duplicated. In addition, they are less likely to move on to a competitor, provided they are treated and compensated fairly. By viewing older job candidates in this positive light, and exuding it, a more meaningful and useful interview results.

That age should be considered an asset, rather than a negative factor, when hiring is demonstrated by a study conducted by psychologists David A. Waldman and Bruce J. Avolio, of the State University of New York at Binghamton. Their conclusions, published in the February 1986 issue of *Journal of Applied Psychology*, evolved after having analyzed a series of surveys, conducted between 1940 and 1983, that measured objective units of productivity. They concluded that older employees were more likely to perform at higher levels than were younger employees in similar positions. I believe their opinion is just as valid today as it ever was.

What is the definition of "older worker?" It's all relative. A 40-year-old job candidate is an older worker when viewed by a 30-year-old interviewer. A 60-year-old, from the vantage point of youth, is supposed to retire, not be looking for a job.

Employees of any age want their jobs to be challenging. They want, and deserve, to function in an atmosphere that is conducive to healthy, productive work, that pays fairly, and that values their contributions. Unfortunately, there are employers who view those outside the mainstream of candidates—older, female, racial or religious minority—as deserving less. The salient fact is that no employee who can get the job done should be treated less fairly than others.

The American Association of Retired Persons (AARP) recommends that companies looking to attract older, more experienced employees consider the following:

- Accommodate physical limitations, including minor modifications to the work site or job. (This is now a law.)
- Examine the possibility of flexible hours, job sharing, and home-based jobs.
- Offer desirable benefits, including medical coverage, life insurance, sick leave, and paid vacations and holidays.
- Make it clear in help-wanted advertisements that experience is valued. This is not meant to condone reverse discrimination; a younger candidate with the requisite skills should not be overlooked in order to hire older workers. At the very least, however, do not structure ads that place a subtle, yet pointed added value on youth.

The Disabled

Discrimination against the disabled has captured national attention with the passing of the American with Disabilities Act (ADA), which took effect on July 26, 1992. Basically, the Act forbids companies with more than 25 employees to discriminate against the disabled in hiring, compensation, or advancement, and requires that these companies provide reasonable accommodations for disabled workers.

Currently, approximately 30 percent of the estimated 14 million disabled Americans of working age are in the workplace. I predict millions more becoming employed as employers begin to create a more habitable environment for them. The ADA is the voice that speaks clearly for disabled Americans, reaffirming a cause for which the disabled have fought for years—equal status in the workplace. It ensures that persons with disabilities or serious illnesses are not to be easily dismissed; employers must make provisions for them.

The implications of the ADA are numerous, although they remain ambiguous to employers because of the Act's language. For example, the ADA states that employers will need to provide disabled employees with "reasonable accommodation," although "reasonable" is not defined, leaving that clarification to the discretion of the courts when actions brought under the new Act are heard.

Many businesspeople consider the ADA to be legislation that places a severe and undue burden on American industry. Certain forces in the business community and in Congress are attempting to, at the very least, modify its demands. But as this book is written, the ADA is the law of the land, and it will have considerable impact on the overall workplace environment across the United States.

In her book, *Disability Etiquette in the Workplace*, Patricia Morrissey, vice-president of the Washington-based Employment Advisory Services Inc., offers the following advice on how companies can easily comply with the Act's provisions:

- When interviewing a person with disabilities, it's important that the interviewer know the essential functions of the job, ask questions related to those essential functions, and focus upon the disabled person's skill level as it relates to the job.

- Treat disabled job candidates as you do all other candidates. Maintain eye contact; it establishes that you're comfortable with and interested in them as people, not in their disabilities.

  Naturally, interviewing techniques might have to be altered depending upon the disability. If the candidate is hearing-impaired, modifications of the interview setting should be considered.

- Once a disabled person is hired, information access might also need to be modified. For example, a hearing-impaired employee may need the use of a "buddy system," someone to explain announcements made over the company's public address system, or what's said in a meeting. Likewise, the configuration of desks, photocopy machines and mailboxes may have to be changed to better accommodate an employee in a wheelchair.

But all such considerations address the underlying issue of *sensitivity*. Similar to corporate programs to educate employees on the issue of sexual harassment, companies reap rewards by instituting educational projects to sensitize nondisabled employees on how to better accommodate and work with their disabled colleagues.

Some larger companies have been in the forefront of accommodating for the disabled for years. For example:

- AT&T has been training managers and instituting programs in this area for a quarter-century, and was one of the companies that actually helped the government formulate the bill.

- Nike has rewritten its job descriptions, is training supervisory personnel to comply with the law, and is heralding the accomplishments of the disabled.

- Ford has an ongoing education program for supervisors and tests them on a regular basis.

- Pacific Telesis has restructured its employment interviewing techniques to better serve the disabled and adapts tools to their needs.

- U.S. West actively recruits the disabled through campus and community organizations and modifies equipment for them.

Smaller companies, of course, often do not have staff necessary to create and implement broad-based programs to meet and exceed the Act's requirements, although some smaller firms have been in the vanguard of rights for the disabled for a long time. A prime example is Kreonite, Inc., a Kansas manufacturer of darkroom equipment, with $30 million in annual sales. Kreonite hired its first disabled worker more than 20 years ago and currently has a full-time employee on-staff to assist disabled employees. According to Larry Burd, senior vice-president for manufacturing, the disabled are not hired because the company is altruistic—they are hired for their abilities. By his own admission, the company lost many of its disabled workers a few years ago because "we patronized and segregated them." Today, under new and enlightened policies, Kreonite's workforce of disabled men and women is loyal and tends to stay with the firm for many years.

The time and money provided to establish a lawful and compassionate company policy for disabled workers is well spent. Enlightened educational programs, coupled with honest and ethical employment standards, certainly cost less than defending a policy that chooses to ignore both, which often results in costly litigation. Companies seeking to honor the specifics, as well as the spirit of antidiscrimination employment law, should confer with legal counsel on a regular basis to ensure that day-to-day operations are free from discriminatory behavior. In the case of the disabled, health insurance plans should be reviewed to ensure that they don't discriminate; medical histories and exams should not be undertaken prior to offering a job; and job descriptions should focus on the main requirements and omit fringe duties that would rule out the disabled.

REVIEW ALL EMPLOYMENT POLICIES TO PREVENT DISCRIMINATION AND AVOID LAWSUITS

In order to avoid charges of discrimination of all kinds—the disabled, gender, race, religion, age, or ethnic background—every company should take a careful look whenever changes are made to employee handbooks, hiring criteria, promotion policies, pension plans, or any other factors that directly impact their employees. Anything *written* that touches upon the conduct and well-being of employees should be scrutinized by legal counsel.

Similarly, verbal promises made to an employee should be considered carefully in advance. Even a comment as seemingly innocuous as, "We expect you'll have a rewarding career with us that will last for many years," can be held against a company in the event the employee files a lawsuit after being dismissed.

An unfortunate situation? Of course. America's aggressive litigious climate has spawned the need for such caution by every employer, and that means planning ahead. How many employers have been "burned" when, deciding to fire an employee, they suddenly begin stuffing that individual's file with negative performance reviews? That's too late. Any court will look askance at such conduct.

Future chapters will more closely examine ways to reduce legal vulnerability in such areas as checking references, interviewing, drafting application forms, promoting employees, salary structure, employment contracts, and dismissing employees who aren't performing adequately. For now, acknowledge that some forward thinking, planning, and implementation of employment policies can go a long way toward heading off future legal entanglements. Such anticipation will keep a company out of the courtroom, but more important, it makes a company a fair and attractive employer in its community.

5

WHO IS MR./MS. RIGHT?

Identifying Outstanding Job Candidates

"Those who hire people better than themselves do better."

If you and others in your firm view the hiring process as being a matter of "I'll know the right person when I see him or her," you aren't alone.

The tendency to hire on instinct—rather than using a more pragmatic, structured approach—is widespread. Our own (Robert Half International) studies show that approximately 86 percent of managers make their hiring decision within a few minutes of meeting the candidate. Of course, this decision is made after having also evaluated that person's educational and professional background provided in a resume and perhaps from receiving recommendations from friends and business associates.

There is a valid reason for this instinctive response. As humans, we react viscerally to other human beings. We perk up on meeting a pleasant, confident, positive person, for example. Since we spend most of our waking hours at work and are surrounded by professional colleagues, we want them to possess such attributes. It's only natural to respond more to an individual's persona, than to a series of cognitive calculations.

Does this represent the best way to "hire smart?" Although it will always be part of the decision-making process, to depend exclusively upon instinct when hiring is, in my opinion, asking for trouble.

DON'T HIRE ON INSTINCT

First impressions can be misleading. Everyone in the personnel services field has seen candidates who, at first blush, make a tremendous impression. They've honed their presentational skills to a fine edge, possess all sorts of seemingly relevant knowledge, and are never at a loss for the right words. They're likable; after all, who dislikes a likable person? In many cases, they've worked for many employers during their careers. Why shouldn't they have? They're good and experienced at landing jobs.

These same people might be 100 percent genuine, exactly the type you want to fill a key job. The dream candidates. Mr. or Ms. Right. Then again, maybe they aren't. Maybe, because of a lack of structure in the hiring process, they've simply arrived at the right time. It's been a long search. You're anxious to fill the job and get on with other things. Enough is enough.

On the other hand, what about that good candidate who arrived early in the search and has been forgotten because of a lack of structure in how the search was conducted? It's my experience that the first in a field of many candidates to be interviewed, is seldom offered the job. That person is simply forgotten in the maze of more recent candidates.

Were the specs for the position considered carefully, and heeded? Does the candidate really need all that education or that many years of experience in a narrow niche?

Did hidden bias come into play when making the decision? I know of a manager who turned down an otherwise excellent candidate because he parted his hair in the middle. Years ago, another manager refused to hire anyone overweight because "all fat people steal."

HIRE OUTSTANDING EMPLOYEES

Was there a real effort to hire the best, even though that person might eventually pose a threat to the executive doing the hiring? The great retailer J.C. Penney once said, "I will have no man work for me who doesn't have the capacity to become a partner," a sentiment echoed by the inscription on Andrew Carnegie's tombstone, "Here lies a man who knew how to enlist the service of better men than himself." Less secure managers, perhaps unconsciously, hire those who don't pose a threat to their jobs. Astute human resources professionals are aware of this potential and do what they can to keep outstanding candidates in the running with such employers.

The long-term ramifications for companies that allow this ingredient to influence hiring decisions is profound. David Ogilvy, the bigger-than-life genius who helped shape advertising as we know it today, once entered a board meeting at the agency he founded, Ogilvy & Mather, carrying a box filled with Russian dolls. Placing one doll in front of each director, he said, "This represents you." He told them to open the dolls. They did as instructed, removing each of the increasingly smaller dolls until reaching the last and smallest one. In it was a note that said, in part, "If you always hire people who are smaller than you, we shall become a company of dwarfs. If you always hire people bigger than you, we shall become a company of giants."

To ensure that your hiring practices bring in outstanding employees, ask yourself the following questions:

- Did the "cloning phenomenon" play an undue role in choosing a candidate over all others? We naturally like to surround ourselves with people who reflect our attributes, but that can be counterproductive when staffing a company. Hiring clones of ourselves precludes injecting new ideas, which every company needs.

- Was the search too limited in terms of the sources plumbed for the right candidate? That is, was the search restricted to only certain schools? Did you use only newspaper advertising at the exclusion of networking, advertise through more unconventional, targeted media, or use a professional search organization specializing in the sort of candidate that was needed?

- Were the interviews conducted in a proper atmosphere, free from distractions and interruptions? When each interview concluded, was there a system through which relevant comments, impressions, and reactions could be noted? (This is a way to remember the pluses of candidates interviewed early in the hiring process.)

- Were references checked thoroughly? Was only the candidate's list used, or did you go beyond it? If a reference check fails to bring up *something* unfavorable, it hasn't been thorough enough. Everyone has something negative in their working lives, and someone who will have something to say that isn't complimentary. This means that the "perfect person" doesn't exist, any more than does the perfect job.

Does that mean settling? Within certain parameters, yes, depending on your definition of "settling."

Every company wants to hire "stars," those individuals who will become innovative leaders and make a large contribution to the company's future success. Can they be identified in advance? To some extent, but this brings us back to hiring-by-instinct. Although a modicum of gut reaction is to be expected and even welcomed when making a hiring decision, there are ways to codify what inherently is a reactive decision. These involve evaluating two intangible aspects of candidates that transcend the "hard qualifications" of education, knowledge, experience, and skills. They are the candidates' (1) level of self-esteem and (2) demonstrable communication and interpersonal abilities.

Evaluating a Candidate's Self-Esteem

A recent study conducted by David Moment and Abraham Zaleznik at the Harvard Business School underscored the importance of self-esteem in the workplace. They studied people in middle and upper management positions by asking co-workers to rate these executives on their ability to present ideas, lead a discussion, take on a leadership role, and develop friendships.

The findings were broken down into four categories:

- Those who rated high in each area were labeled "stars."
- Those who were high in everything but the congenial categories were labeled "technical specialists."
- Those who scored high only in the congenial areas were designated "social specialists."
- The rest were termed the *underchosen*.

The researchers determined that the stars differed from the others in only one significant way. They had immense confidence in themselves. They were perceived as being efficient, competent, and able to meet any challenge they faced. They believed in what they could accomplish, given virtually any situation. They had heightened self-esteem.

The sort of successful executives defined by the Harvard study will conjure for some an image of overly aggressive, egotistical blowhards. Those who see them in that light suffer the same sort of prejudice as the person who views overweight people as being inherently dishonest. It isn't difficult to ascertain whether job candidates possess a quiet, steady faith in themselves or are of the insufferable variety. People with a healthy sense of self-worth carry themselves with more poise and exude realistic confidence.

From the standpoint of making a hiring decision, however, nothing better indicates a candidate's confidence than his or her view of the world in general. Are they optimistic of pessimistic? Do they view the proverbial glass as half empty or half full? People with a positive world-view are infinitely more likely to be happier, more productive, and more efficient. They are easier to motivate, are quicker to learn and adapt to a variety of situations, and, in general, have greater potential to become stars in a company. In line with this approach to evaluating competing candidates for a job, Robert Half International has always suggested to corporate clients that when all else is equal, choose the person who most wants the job.

EVALUATING A CANDIDATE'S COMMUNICATION AND INTERPERSONAL SKILLS

The second, less tangible factor to be considered is a candidate's verbal and written communication skills, along with the ability to interact with colleagues, to inspire confidence from them, and to function as a team player. This can be determined to some extent from previous responsibilities as indicated on a resume, careful questioning during interviews, and checking references.

Whether a candidate is verbally secure is evident during interviews, but look beyond that. How do others respond to the candidate's approach to people? How does the receptionist or an assistant react to the candidate? Was he or she courteous or contemptuous toward this lower-level employee? Would that receptionist or assistant enjoy working on a daily basis with the candidate? Receptionists and administrative assistants have been known to sink a candidate's chances more often than most people realize. They should be listened to for exactly that reason. Candidates might have impeccable credentials and impressive interviewing skills, but if those credentials don't mesh with a smoothly functioning team, they end up having little value to the company.

Robert Half International isn't alone in calling for interpersonal relations to rank high in employer priority. In 1990 our survey of 200 executives selected from the 1,000 largest companies in the United States indicated that 74 percent felt there was a *shortage* of candidates with these skills. In addition to our survey, dozens of similar studies consistently rank interpersonal and communications skills at the top of the list of desired traits in job candidates.

HOW TO EVALUATE A CANDIDATE'S "INTANGIBLE" CHARACTERISTICS

Earlier, I characterized certain traits as "intangible," but they don't necessarily have to remain so. A hiring manager can find tangible proof by asking the following questions:

- Was the resume written with care?
- Was the resume proofread for typographical errors and awkward syntax?
- Does the resume mean what the candidate intends it to mean, and is it filled with vague language and unsubstantiated claims?
- Is the cover letter accompanying the resume well written or ineptly crafted?
- Are answers to interview questions direct and cogent, or rambling and confusing?

With careful attention to these matters—a commitment to incorporating them into the decision-making process—they become less intangible and are less likely to be ignored.

When faced with a choice of hiring a person who is perceived as representing the weakest in a field of strong candidates, or a person who is the strongest in a weak field, the former is generally the better choice. This doesn't necessarily mean "settling" in the pejorative sense of the word. Remember, the field of highly qualified candidates has dwindled, and it will continue to shrink. Companies that have poised themselves to attract the cream of the crop naturally will succeed in landing employees who are coveted by many. For companies not yet to that point, choosing someone from a field of good people, but who doesn't rank on top, can still represent a quality employee. Given the proper motivation and opportunity, such people are likely to improve and to help a company prosper.

How trainable is the candidate? This addresses the question of how much experience a candidate brings to the company. Hiring a thoroughly experienced person negates the need for much training, but that same person can prove to be intractable when presented with new ideas. On the other hand, a less experienced person might be more malleable, an advantage for a management interested in shaping people to its way of doing business. It doesn't matter which approach is taken as long as it's thoroughly discussed and resolved before specifications for the job are finalized, an area that receives less attention than it deserves.

6

SPELLING IT OUT

Writing Job Descriptions

"Long copy is skimmed, short copy is read."

As suggested in previous chapters, job descriptions must be skillfully crafted before the hiring process can begin. Is this easier said than done? Not if a few basic rules are followed.

KEEP THE JOB DESCRIPTION BRIEF

To many people, clear, detailed writing translates into the need to create longer documents. More words, they feel, will convey more useful information. In fact, the opposite is true. Although it may be harder to get across a point with fewer words than with many, the result is much more effective when accomplished. A good job description will have been written, edited, rewritten, edited again, and then again until it spells out in clear, concise language what the job *really* demands.

I believe that a job specification should fit comfortably on one page. If it runs longer than that, it's probably too specific. An effective job description should include

- All the basic skills required, but be limited to those that are truly necessary to get the job done. Sometimes forgotten are "soft skills," such as ability to communicate verbally or in writing, to interact closely as a team player, or to demonstrate supervisory skills over a fluctuating number of specialists.

- A clear picture of what is expected in the way of deadlines, regularly scheduled written and verbal progress reports, expense tracking, company hours (including the need to extend them in times of increased workload), and other requirements that are better explained early in the hiring process, rather than later
- The name and title of the person to whom the employee will report, and others with whom the person will closely interact
- Salary and benefits. If at all possible, pay a little more than market. If there is a lot of turnover at your company, consider paying a lot more. As may happen in small firms, the hiring person sometimes feels as though salaries come directly out of his or her own pocket, resulting in a pattern of salary "lowballing." Getting what you pay for has particular applicability to hiring and staffing. Your objective is to get the *best* possible person for the job, and the best people know they're good and deserve a decent salary for their skills.

DESCRIBE THE JOB ACCURATELY

Like all good writing, it's the thinking behind it that counts. The most skilled writer of job descriptions will fail if the thought behind what he or she is writing—the analyses of the job itself—is faulty. Too many job descriptions call for education, skills, and experience far beyond what the job requires.

Frequently, an unrealistic salary accompanies these inflated job descriptions. This represents the biggest problem human resources professionals have in matching candidates to jobs. A company can't insist that an individual have a Ph.D., yet offer a salary more appropriate for a high school graduate. This is not to say that all candidates with the stipulated requisites would reject the offer. Even though the employer might succeed in hiring a person with the ballooned credentials, the employer has laid the groundwork for rapid turnover: the revolving door.

On the other side of the coin, there are employers who minimize job specs in order to hire someone at a low salary, but then crank up demands once the employee starts working. The results? There goes that revolving door again. Still other employers make a position sound as though it involves considerable managerial responsibility, when in reality it is a mundane, boring job with little or no managing involved.

A good job description begins with honesty. "Fudging" a job description in order to attract candidates who otherwise would not be interested, is to court disaster. Reality soon sets in, and the employee recognizes the deception. Misleading job descriptions are akin to candidates landing jobs based on fraudulent resumes. They may find the jobs,but their inadequacies soon surface.

Ironically, my associates and I have known employers who go to excess in downplaying the appeal of a given job and the potential for growth. Because we've had a long-term relationship with many of them, we *know* that the position is better than indicated in the job description and that the company has a good track record of promoting from within. Getting that across to a good candidate who returns from an interview with a negative view of the company and job isn't always easy.

DON'T RELY ON DEPARTING EMPLOYEES TO WRITE THE NEW JOB DESCRIPTION

You can ask the departing employee to prepare a detailed outline of what he or she did on the job. But also look at this employee's application blank and resume at the time of employment. There's a strong possibility that this individual did not have experience in *everything* that he or she has been doing at the present time—other than basic skills and training that would ordinarily be required. For example, a controller would ordinarily be an accomplished accountant and have managerial experience. This person, if capable, should be able to learn about the industry and the office and accounting systems. I purposely oversimplified this to make it clear that almost everyone who comes in as a new employee, if competent, is able to use their skills and their training to handle the position effectively. If you're convinced that the candidate is willing to do the job, and has the ability, everything else becomes much less important.

The employee who is quitting tends to overcomplicate the requirements, and consciously or unconsciously may not be looking to hire the best person for the job for two reasons:

1. Ego. The tendency of wanting to be missed because *she was the best controller the company ever had.*

2. Hedging. If the new and "better" job doesn't work out, she'd like to be able to re-apply for her old job.

Unless you have an excellent reason to let the departing person participate in creating the job specifications and conducting interviews, don't do it. It may be the easy way out, but that shouldn't be your goal.

MODIFY THE JOB DESCRIPTION IF NECESSARY

Finally, we urge employers not to consider job descriptions as set in stone. They will have lasting value if properly conceived and drafted, but they should be flexible enough so that aspects of them can be altered if the right person comes along. A sterling prospect, deficient in a single area called for in a job description, should not be overlooked. Is that aspect of the job really as important as stated in the description? If so, can the deficiency be corrected through company training or company-sponsored education?

At Robert Half International, we've seen too many otherwise superb matches between candidate and employer lost as a result of undue rigidity on the employer's part. We're not advocating a lowering of standards, but if, in your judgment, a candidate has the ability and willingness to do the job, this person should be seriously considered for the position.

7

SEEK AND YE SHALL FIND

Finding the Best Job Candidates

"Always keep your eyes open to find hard-to-find employees."

Despite business downturns, there are always thousands of jobs to be filled each year. When business is down, many people are out of work and looking. So, why is there a problem finding qualified candidates to fill open positions during tough times?

The problem is that the "cream" of the employed know they have superior skills to offer and have become more selective in choosing companies to which they will apply. Contrasting this, if companies are concentrating on downsizing, recruitment efforts have usually been placed on the back burner.

Periods of poor business are not necessarily the time to cut back on seeking outstanding people, any more than it is for a company to stop advertising its products and services. Companies that continue to advertise during hard times protect brand identification and market share for when times are good again. Similarly, companies that continue to seek *outstanding* employees are infinitely better prepared to prosper when the economic cycle takes an upturn.

There are many ways to seek and identify good employees. Some are traditional and stale; they comprise a staple of recruiting techniques a company may have used for years, but should be refined to meet new challenges. Others are original and not time-tested, but are being used more often in the overall recruiting mix. Two of these, described at the end of this chapter, are rehiring former employees, and changing attitudes toward unemployed workers.

ENCOURAGE EMPLOYEE REFERRALS

More companies are asking their employees to refer candidates for employment. It makes sense. Employees have much to gain by being responsible for an infusion of new, productive talent, and they have a lot to lose by recommending marginal people to fill new jobs.

This is a staffing trend supported by numerous studies. One, the *Hiring and Firing Survey*, published in 1990 by the Administrative Management Society (AMS), surveyed 255 companies. The majority reported relying more heavily on referrals from employees, and lessening their dependency on the more traditional avenue of employment advertising. The study showed that a large majority of companies surveyed had increased their hiring of word-of-mouth referrals provided by current employees. At the same time, the utilization of newspaper "help-wanted" ads had declined.

This trend of looking inward for good employees will undoubtedly grow. The advantages are numerous, including holding down recruitment costs.

Companies that have beefed up recruiting through internal sources have formalized the process. They've instituted programs in which employees receive recognition and reward if a person they have recommended is eventually hired. This can take the form of a cash bonus, dinner for two, an extra vacation day with pay, or a salute in the employee newsletter, on bulletin boards, or in letters of commendation from top management.

While the value of using current employees to bring in new people appears to be almost axiomatic, this method is not without problems. These stem from entrenched corporate philosophies that too many friends working at the same place causes too much socializing. On the contrary, it's been my experience that good workers bring in good workers.

The prime example is the age-old rule—one we consider anachronistic—set by many companies against employing two (or more) people from the same family. The specifics vary from company to company: no husband and wife may work for the same firm; a husband and wife may work for the same firm, but not in the same department; a husband and wife may be hired, provided one doesn't supervise the other; no husband and wife may be hired, but other family relationships are okay; no kinship closer than first cousins will be allowed; no unmarried couples living as married; and other restrictions.

The reasons for these conditions are well meaning and are founded on a belief that it is more difficult for family members to *manage* other family members. In addition, potential conflicts of interest, fear of being accused of favoritism, and a resulting weakening of morale are often cited as factors.

These prohibitions don't hold up to common sense any more than do reasons that restrict hiring to a certain age group, gender, ethnic background, or schooling. Why exclude other members of a family because of arbitrary rules that are, in turn, based on arbitrary assumptions? Carrying this illogic even further, a company may presume dissension if a family member is dismissed.

PROMOTE FROM WITHIN

Another employment trend is an increasing willingness to promote from within. It has long been known in management circles that looking first to those on-staff to fill new openings is good for employee morale. Employees who see themselves passed over for promotions—perhaps automatically ruled out simply because they're doing too good a job where they are—are bound to become resentful. Knowing this, why have so many otherwise smart companies routinely looked outside to fill jobs?

One answer is a belief (based, for the most part, on a myth) that in order to fill an important job, you *must* look outside for the right candidates. They represent "new blood," new ideas. There's a certain validity to this, of course. Companies that preclude hiring new people run the risk of becoming stagnant, just as hiring only clones of employees already on-board can produce inertia.

Many people seeking career advancement harbor similar beliefs. They assume that greater opportunity exists only outside present employment. Often, an exploration of opportunities within the place of current employment uncovers greater potential for growth, but the employee has to get past the myth—and resulting belief—that change equals opportunity.

As with employee referral of candidates, there are obvious advantages to promoting (including moving laterally to take better advantage of skills and interests) from within. The person already knows the company's ins-and-outs and has acclimated to its corporate culture. Often, awarding such an employee a new and more attractive title can achieve much.

If promoting from within is to be an effective part of a company's recruiting strategy, it should be formalized. In too many instances, job openings are learned about through the infamous grapevine. To depend on this method places many workers at a distinct disadvantage. Only those with access to rumors learn of openings and are in a position to apply for them (*lobby for them* might be a more appropriate term under these circumstances).

A systematic process of announcing job openings, coupled with an equally structured and equitable channel of applying for them, levels the field. It gives management the best opportunity to evaluate those in contention. Should no employee qualify and it becomes necessary to look outside to fill a position, those who've been turned down know they were treated fairly, that the company believes in career opportunities, and that there are likely to be other opportunities in the future.

Where the number of internal promotions may be limited, a novel approach called *broad-banding* has lately grown in popularity. Many companies, finding themselves with too many salaried employees worthy of promotion but lacking managerial slots to which to promote them, have instituted programs of monetary reward without change in title. Under this plan, employees know that they do not need to be promoted to new job titles and descriptions in order to climb the corporate pay ladder. In essence, it revises traditional thinking; it pays for an employee's performance rather than for his or her job title. Under this notion, a manager may make a lateral move to an assistant manager's position without sacrificing salary. Some employees might even be paid more than their supervisors. It's an interesting idea that is being experimented with by a number of firms.

CONDUCT CAMPUS RECRUITING

Obtaining the "right" education has always been considered a prime indicator of future success. Presumably, men and women with undergraduate and advanced degrees from prestigious universities are prepared to apply what they've learned to a company's business interests, eventually reaching high positions of management.

That assumption retains a certain level of validity. Education—from any source—equips people to know more and, by extension, to contribute more. Our competitive diminution in the global economy of the 1990s has resulted, in part, from an educational system that has fallen behind some other nations, especially in such critical areas as science and math.

The emphasis on education, particularly the methods for evaluating it, have changed, however, as the needs of American industry have changed. Education can no longer be counted on as the indicator of a person's future success.

Graduating from a prestigious university will open certain doors, but once through them, it doesn't necessarily translate into job performance. It never has. Given the current need to accomplish more with fewer people, companies cannot afford the luxury of "carrying" highly educated, less productive people.

A survey taken by Empire State Poll queried 400 graduates of two universities (one prestigious, the other less so) 15 years after they had graduated. The results were as interesting as they were unexpected. The conclusion was that people's attitudes about success and how to achieve it played an important role in actually succeeding. On the other hand, graduate degrees and grade point averages had no bearing upon ultimate career success. In fact, they sometimes had a negative effect.

Respondents to the survey listed, in order of importance, the attributes they felt contributed to career success:

1. Personal work style and habits, quality of skills and knowledge, and quality of work

2. Ability to conform, loyalty to an employer, appearance, and sharing an employer's values and goals

3. Background characteristics, including gender, socioeconomic background, ethnicity, and religion

4. Education, including the reputation of the university attended, and grades

While the third item is discouraging in light of what we would hope would be a more enlightened view of eliminating discrimination in the workplace, the fact that education ranked last of the four criteria is important, especially for human resource professionals. Evidently management, after too many years of placing undue emphasis on the educational background of job candidates, is beginning to look for other qualifications that have more direct bearing on job performance and career success.

The Empire State Poll revealed an interesting dichotomy between success and income. On the average, those who graduated from a prestigious school earned as much as $20,000 more per year than counterparts who came out of less prestigious institutions. At the same time, individuals who focused during their undergraduate years on a curriculum directly related to the skills needed to begin a career, earned $5,000 more per year than those who took a more generalized educational path—regardless of the reputation of the school attended.

In some cases, education can actually work *against* an individual. According to the same survey, those who held an MBA were, on the average, paid $10,000 less than those who had attained only under-graduate degrees. The former earned $32,000 annually, while the latter earned $42,000. Why?

Many respondents felt that going after an MBA was wasted time. Because there are so many people these days with an MBA, its value has diminished by virtue of supply and demand.

The major reason for this negative feeling about MBAs had to do with preferring that employees learn through on-the-job training, rather than through extended academic experiences. The ability to handle the demands of a specific job was significantly more important to those employers in the survey than was theoretical knowledge.

The extent to which campus recruiting fits into a company's overall staffing plans depends on numerous factors, the most obvious being how many entry-level slots are to be filled and what educational credentials must be possessed by those filling them. However, the reality of these economic times, coupled with the increasing global impact of business, necessitates factoring in other less tangible, more intellectual determinations and raises a number of questions:

- Has the recent college graduate become a casualty of financial reality? Can today's lean-and-mean companies afford to train graduates over a period of months, often years, as opposed to hiring more seasoned, experienced candidates who can be up-and-running sooner?

- Does the advantage of being able to shape such raw, untested, more malleable talent to a company's ways of doing things compensate for losing productivity early-on?

- Does the fact that most recent college graduates have not established serious community and family ties, thus allowing them greater flexibility to travel or relocate, tip the balance in their favor over more settled individuals with built-in restrictions?

- What about the "maturity factor?" In the high-flying decades past, companies could afford to wait for promising, but immature, young people to grow into their jobs and develop career skills. Is that luxury still an option?

- Have the criteria for choosing from among academe's best and brightest kept pace with reality? Is undue emphasis still being placed on grade point averages and the perceived prestige of a given institution? Has company policy for judging the relative worth of competing graduates instead been re-thought and revised to reflect contemporary needs?

- Do advanced degrees, particularly MBAs, carry weight beyond what they actually represent in terms of productivity, and the ability to evaluate the future worth of individuals possessing them?

- Is a company's campus recruiting policy based on a tradition of seeking talent only from a small selection of schools that reflect top management's idea of where good employees are nurtured. Has it instead been refined and expanded to include a wider variety of good sources?

The answers to all these questions are found through a diligent and systematic review of hiring policies and how well they've served you. Specifically, try to determine whether employees from prestigious universities have produced more and better output than those from schools with lesser reputations and whether employees with high grade point averages have outperformed their colleagues.

Like a regular review of a company's legal practices in hiring, the educational criteria upon which hiring decisions are made must also be periodically scrutinized. Failing to do so invites perpetuating hiring decisions that might not be in the best interest of the company.

SOLICIT PERSONAL RECOMMENDATIONS—BUT BE CAUTIOUS

Unlike candidate referrals from current employees—where the employee has much to lose, or gain, from recommending the right person—candidates who are referred by a friend of a friend can prove to be more problematic.

The scenario is this: You, a manager looking to fill an opening on your staff, play golf or tennis with a friend. You casually mention the opening. Your friend knows the perfect person for the job—the daughter of a friend's friend. And so the process begins.

It's assumed that 60 percent of job openings are never advertised, and because most people find jobs through networking, and since you, a busy person, would prefer to solve this staffing problem outside traditional recruitment channels, this daughter of a friend's friend sounds *perfect*. After all, she has been recommended by someone you like and trust. This is a candidate certainly worth pursuing.

The complications arise if she is not as qualified as others who might come out of a candidate pool tapped through advertising, the use of a personnel services firm, or some other method. Because of your friendship with the source, there could be embarrassment in not hiring her. If you feel obligated to hire her for this reason, you end up with a less capable employee when you could have had someone with better credentials.

No matter what the source of the referral, every candidate for a job should be evaluated by the same stringent criteria, including diligent reference checking, that is applied to all candidates. To do less is to shortchange your company's future. When it comes to personal recommendations, trust—but verify.

ADVERTISE IN THE CLASSIFIEDS

Despite the fact that most jobs are *not* filled through advertising, it still remains one of the primary vehicles for filling them. Using advertising to fill job openings can create, depending upon a company's needs and human resources capability, the proverbial good news–bad news scenario.

If the advertisement is well written and properly placed, the response might be overwhelming in sheer number of applicants, particularly in days of high unemployment. This means, of course, that you have a deep pool of candidates from which to choose (the good news). It also can mean the backbreaking, confusing chore of weeding out the promising candidates from many unusable submissions (the bad news).

Unfortunately, the writing of employment ads has not progressed far beyond considering it a mechanical chore lacking in creativity and urgency, a task to be performed by rote, often quickly and without much thought. Instead, the writing of employment advertising should be approached in the same way as any other ad, whether for cars or ketchups or cold drinks. The idea, after all, is to create an advertisement that *sells*. If an employment ad does nothing but list job specs and requisite skills—often with incomprehensible abbreviations—it will not sell anyone except a large number of the unemployed who answer any ad in their field, and even some ads that have nothing to do with their field.

The purpose of a good employment ad is to entice the best people to respond, including those currently employed who may reply because the job it offers appears to be a good career move.

The "sell" in an employment ad has less to do with the job and more to do with the company that submits it. This refers back to Chapter 2, which discussed the inherent hiring advantage companies enjoy when they're known to be good places to work. The mere mention of their names causes the employed and unemployed alike to take notice. Like package-goods companies that have developed brand loyalty for their products, employers with a solid reputation for treating their employees fairly, for paying competitive wages, and for offering a decent benefits package enjoy a similar competitive edge, namely loyalty to the company by its employees and those who would like to be its employees.

Create Effective Ads

Whether a company has achieved a good reputation or not, employment advertising should be considered carefully from the standpoint of "selling" the company as a good place to work. All effective advertising offers benefits to the reader: "Cuts your housecleaning time in half;" "Lowers your energy bills;" "Gets more miles to the gallon;" "The lowest fares to California." Employment advertising should strive to do the same. Ads for a job opening should be written using positive, yet accurate, descriptions of the position being offered and the benefits to the person who ultimately fills it, but don't promise things you may not be able or willing to fulfill.

Why should top-notch talent respond to your ad? Because the ad promotes the company's strong points. For example:

- If the company is prospering, crow about it: "Company has grown 30 percent a year for the past three years."
- If the company's location offers advantages, they should be highlighted: "Beautiful offices near all transportation."
- If promotion from within has created the job, point that out: "Incumbent was recently promoted to vice president."

Those who view the writing of employment advertising as a mechanical process will immediately counter by saying that every word in an ad costs money. No argument there, but good advertising demands choosing the right words and thoughts. If a company can boast of such pluses as mentioned in the examples, it makes marketing sense to stress those accomplishments and benefits, and to delete other facts that do not have equally inherent appeal. Remember, you are not simply looking to generate countless responses. What you want is for the ad to prompt a response from the best candidates, regardless of their current employment situation.

Describe the Job Clearly

Avoid the temptation to go overboard with abbreviations, as in this ad:

C/UNIXP/A

4+yrs exp w/PC sys in M/F environ. Kno structured techs & xposure to C, UNIX, 4GLs. Exc career oppty w/prestge co.

Classified advertising has created a whole sub-language. Those who've learned it can be inordinately fond of using it. It has its place, of course, but it shouldn't be used in an attempt to cram a lot of information into an ad when more salient information could be spelled out.

Skilled writers of employment advertising are able to make a position sound attractive without being specific enough to alert the competition to actual compensation and benefits being offered by their companies. Their working creed might be summed up as being vague as possible, but only as specific as necessary.

Employment advertising pros also have a way of leaving little doubt that the background and references of candidates will be thoroughly checked without coming right out and stating it. With the number of "exaggerated" resumes being submitted these days, anything to lessen the likelihood of attracting dishonest candidates is time and money saved. As part of the image building described in Chapter 2, companies that establish themselves as thorough when it comes to checking references will automatically have bettered their chances of avoiding submissions by less-than-honest job seekers.

Some companies, in an effort to fill positions as quickly as possible, overstate the potentials of jobs in their ads. In effect, an employment ad is a *company's* resume that is submitted to potential employees. An ad, like a resume, should, as the old song goes, "accentuate the positive and deccentuate the negative," but always within the boundaries of accuracy and honesty. The fastest way to fail to retain good people (the subject of Part II of this book) is to hire them under false pretenses for jobs that don't match up to pre-employment promises.

Don't Use Blind Ads

The debate over whether to identify a company in an employment ad, or to run a so-called blind ad in which the employer is not named, will always be around.

Even for companies that do not enjoy the envious reputation as good places to work, blind employment ads generate considerably less quality response. Currently employed, savvy job seekers do not answer such ads because they might have been run by their own companies or a friend of an executive at their current place of employment.

Advertise in the Appropriate Publication

While the creation of employment advertising has certain unique aspects and demands, it is, after all, advertising. If there is anything destined to improve the effectiveness of employment ads, it will come from the recognition that it, like all advertising, is a creative act designed to interest the right people. At the same time, the choice of media in which to place employment ads must be evaluated carefully.

We are no longer a "general interest" society. The days of most of our information coming from large television networks, and a handful of broad-based magazines and general-interest newspapers, have gone the way of cable TV and the mind-boggling variety of publications that focus on special-interest readership. There is a magazine for every interest, no matter how narrow, as well as targeted radio and television stations.

Still, the employment industry at-large tends to place ads in the tried-and-true, large publications and hope for the best. The reason is simple. It's easier to take this route than to seek out and negotiate with numerous smaller media even though they will more directly reach the best source of candidates to fill specific jobs.

That said, the more traditional media for employment advertising still remain useful when hiring. As any media buyer in any ad agency will testify, you choose the media that is *read by the people you wish to reach*.

For example, a musical instrument manufacturing company seeking a controller might advertise the opening in *The Wall Street Journal* and other mainstream newspapers routinely read by executives seeking new job opportunities. That's a good reason to advertise in such publications. Job seekers expect better jobs to be advertised in them. On the other hand, by advertising the same job in publications read by music buffs and spelling out the qualifications needed to be considered, you stand a good chance of finding a qualified controller who also happens to love the music industry, and who has special knowledge of it in addition to good controller credentials. Of course, it isn't necessary to love an industry in order to be an effective controller, but it helps. Job satisfaction tends to be higher when employees enjoy their work environment, aside from its professional demands.

The choice of which broader-based newspapers and magazines in which to advertise depends, once again, on those candidates you wish to reach. Consider the following choices.

Major newspapers. The advertising sections in major newspapers are read regularly by unemployed job seekers and the employed alike. Many of the latter are cozy in their current positions but wish to monitor their market value, as well as stay alert to career opportunities. These individuals realize that the concept of "in it for life" no longer exists in today's job market. They anticipate changing jobs at least several times during their careers.

The Wall Street Journal. The *Journal* features "The Mart," the daily exchange of available positions. The *Journal* is read nationally and internationally, and it is a highly respected source of executive openings around the world. In addition, the *National Business Employment Weekly* reprints recruitment ads from all editions of *The Wall Street Journal*, plus sells ads directly in certain categories, such as High-Tech, Health Care, the entry-level, and for products and services directed to job hunters.

Regional and local newspapers. These are effective advertising outlets, particularly when geographic considerations are part of the picture. *The New York Times, Los Angeles Times, Chicago Tribune, Washington Post, Boston Globe, Denver Post,* and *San Francisco Chronicle* are among the most read and respected regional papers in the United States.

With each of them, and others around this country, it's important to keep in mind that they not only serve a distinct geographic area, but also tend to reach different audiences with different skills. For example, Los Angeles has a significant number of scientific and engineering professionals working in the defense industry; Boston has a healthy draw of high-tech and computer technology experts; Washington's audience is naturally rife with men and women possessing government and overseas experience; Hartford, Connecticut, is the insurance capital of America; Detroit is the center of the automotive industry; and so on.

An insurance company in Denver will naturally hope to recruit people from that city in order to avoid relocation expense, but the candidate pool of insurance professionals is deeper and wider in Hartford. To restrict the filling of a job to only the local area—when better people can be reached and recruited elsewhere—can prove shortsighted over the long haul.

General-interest business publications. For example, *Barron's, Business Week*, and *Industry Week* are widely read by business-oriented audiences. So are such magazines as *Money, Inc., Fortune, Forbes*, and the *Harvard Business Review*. Because they are not routinely read by active job seekers, advertising in them is costly and there is virtually no employment advertising in them. Unless there is a special reason for using them, they probably should not be considered part of a basic media package.

Career-specific publications. These allow employment advertisers to reach people with specific education and professional skills. Examples include *Advertising Age, American Banker, Chemical Engineering, Purchasing World, Personnel Journal, Management Accounting, Journal of Accountancy, Publishers Weekly*, and hundreds of others. Although they target a more narrowly focused candidate field, many do not reach a broad cross-section. Some are linked to membership in trade associations, and only members receive the magazine. Still other magazines are received, but in a busy world they are laid aside to be read "if and when I have time."

Every advertising campaign to find top people should include such industry publications on the list of potential media. An ad in major newspapers will certainly generate many responses, but adding professional and trade magazines to the media mix might prompt someone of exceptional qualifications to reply.

University publications. These are becoming increasingly popular as advertising vehicles for a variety of products and services. Companies wishing to cut down the cost of in-person campus recruiting might find them productive. The cost is low and readership is motivated.

Tips on Employment Advertising

Whatever approach is taken when advertising jobs, and whatever the philosophy, I urge

- That it be viewed as a creative act, like the writing of *any* advertising—and that it "sell"

- That the choice of media be expanded beyond the usual, and consideration be given to smaller, more targeted media despite the additional work involved

BUILD A PROFESSIONAL NETWORK

Networking is generally thought of as being the purview of job candidates, not companies seeking employees. But it cuts both ways. The advantage of networking to fill jobs—aside from the considerable savings in time and money—is that it begins far in advance of the actual hiring process. Once in place, the dividends of having networked throughout the years can pay off immediately, and repeatedly. However, as with job seekers, building a useful network doesn't "just happen." It takes dedication to the task, and an ongoing effort to build and nurture the network.

In a sense, a human resources department (or any manager) that networks functions in much the same way a personnel service organization does—by keeping close tabs on an industry and its people. Over the course of time, membership in trade and professional associations and community organizations puts companies in touch with a variety of men and women, each of whom is a potential employee.

Like every other aspect of putting into effect a long-term staffing strategy, building and maintaining a network takes time and effort. Just as it has always paid off for men and women who do it in the interest of furthering their careers, it can reap the same benefits for employers.

USE PERSONNEL SERVICE FIRMS

As mentioned in the previous section, personnel recruiters (also known as executive search firms or headhunters) are in the business of maintaining hiring networks and using them to match the right person to the right job. In many cases, creating such networks by a single company's human resources department, as well as other members of management, is simply too time consuming and expensive. This is where utilizing the right personnel services firm can pay dividends.

There are a wide variety of personnel service firms from which to choose. Some are generalists, offering a multitude of job candidates in many broad categories. A good number of them deal primarily with lower-level employees. Other firms that provide general placement services limit themselves to executive positions, without restriction by profession or industry. Still others specialize in selected industries and professions. For example, Robert Half International fills positions in the fields of finance, accounting, banking, and information systems.

Depending on a company's needs, the first decision to be made is whether to work with a personnel services company that specializes or with one that is more generalized. There are obvious advantages in working with specialists, the most important of which is the focus they place on people within a given industry or profession. The better ones maintain that network of contacts with top people in tracking careers, constantly evaluating each individual's background, skills, and needs. They utilize the expertise of their placement counselors, most of whom have come out of the profession in which the firm specializes, to analyze the type of individual best suited for a company and the job opening.

The second decision to be made is whether to go with a "retainer" firm or one that functions on a contingency basis. Traditionally, retainer firms' charges are nonrefundable, and they bill the client for all incurred expenses, including travel and advertising. These costs are paid by the client-company whether or not it actually hires through the retainer firm. Contingency firms, on the other hand, bill the client only when a candidate who was provided through them has actually been hired.

Both retainer and contingency firms recruit candidates who are currently employed and those who are between jobs. Both also accept assignments at virtually any management or professional salary level, maintain pools of potential candidates through networking, and advertise in appropriate media.

Once a particular personnel service has been chosen, careful consideration should be given to its credentials. In a sense, a company "hires" such a firm; the same care should be applied as when hiring an individual employee.

- Ask for references.
- How long has it been in business?
- What is the firm's reputation for ethics? Does it mesh with yours?
- Check with the Better Business Bureau to see if the firm has been the recipient of complaints.
- Ask up-front about fees and refund policies.
- What specific services are offered? Does the firm have national

and international branches that work together to identify the widest array of potential candidates?

- How thorough is the firm in gathering information about the client-company? If it isn't, look elsewhere. A good firm will probe a company's history, its recent and potential growth, recruiting and hiring standards, workplace conditions and culture, and benefits. Any reputable personnel services firm will need to know these things in order to match the right candidate to the job and company and to "sell" the company to the right candidate.

CONSIDER REHIRING FORMER EMPLOYEES

It's always a loss when a good employee decides to leave, but it doesn't have to be permanent. Savvy companies closely track the careers of good former employees. They keep in touch, and when an opening occurs for which the former employee is perfect, that fact is made known to the individual. Perhaps the person's current job isn't working out as anticipated. Maybe the opening at the former employer provides yet another opportunity to advance.

Whatever the reason, former employees can be a good source of talent, provided the employer can get past what some perceive as an awkward situation. (It's my contention that when it comes to properly staffing a company, awkward situations shouldn't stand in the way of success.)

Hiring former employees gives a company the same advantage as converting a temporary worker to full-time. Both are known quantities, which takes much of the guesswork out of the hiring decision. Former employees are familiar with a company's policies, procedures, ethical standards, and culture. They require less training, and they return with additional experience that can enhance their future performance.

Along the same lines, candidates who either chose to accept another offer or were considered second-best to the person actually hired should be reconsidered if a new position opens. Their current situation might not be palatable to them, and they may welcome a "feeler" from the company for which they almost worked.

Our experience at Robert Half International has been that although both sources of potential employees should always be considered, if a former employee is chosen, an honest foundation must be laid before the person actually returns. Thomas Wolfe's observation,

"You can't go home again," can apply, particularly if the former employee has been away for a long time.

Employees sometimes return to find that co-workers have advanced, policies have changed, and new management has been hired. In other words, the job and the company might not be as the former employee remembers. It's best that this person be made aware of any changes *before* being rehired. Similarly, the attitude of a former employee may have changed for any number of reasons.

In addition, many companies are rehiring retirees for part-time duties. These employees also require little or no training costs and are known quantities, and they have likely developed deep-rooted loyalty to the company.

Staffing through any of these somewhat unconventional channels can prove effective. If they can be summed up in a single philosophy, it is that when a company loses good people, for whatever reason, it pays to keep them in mind when filling new jobs. Never slam the door on any employee you're unhappy to see go.

DON'T OVERLOOK THE UNEMPLOYED

Remarkably, there are still many employers in this time of downsizing, mergers, and acquisitions who look askance at job candidates who are out of work because of a company's decision to let them go. There's no particular onus to having been dismissed from a job, provided it wasn't the result of poor job performance (or worse).

A good job candidate should not have to overcome the stigma of being unemployed. Hiring someone who is without employment has certain advantages:

- An unemployed person doesn't have to give notice to an employer or psychologically overcome allegiance to an organization.
- Because accepting a job is not the result of having looked to better current salary and benefits, an unemployed person usually will be willing to accept the same salary they earned earlier, or perhaps less. (Which is not to say that this condition should be exploited as a means of hiring quality people for less than they are worth.)
- References are easier to check when a candidate is not employed.

Keep in mind that these advantages are not cause to look first to the unemployed to fill a position. The best approach to effective hiring is to view *all* candidates with an open mind.

8

A TEMPORARY EXPERIENCE

Hiring Temporary Help

"One way or another, everyone is temporary."

The hiring of temporary workers has gained importance from a number of perspectives. Especially in today's erratic business climate, the benefits are even more abundant.

It wasn't long ago that temporary help was used primarily to fill in for a vacationing or sick employee and to lend a helping hand for seasonal demand. "Temporaries" still provide these needed services. As companies try to evaluate their overall staffing needs, more are factoring in the scheduled use of temporary help in order to maintain a leaner full-time workforce.

Research by Robert Half International, conducted among human resources managers at 200 of the nation's 1,000 largest companies, produced the following data in 1991:

- Eighty-one percent of respondents said they preferred to see their company slightly understaffed, relative to its workload, at any given time.

- Seventy-eight percent of those same respondents said their companies were more likely to use temporary workers for specialized positions than they were during the previous three years.

Given the findings of this research, it is no surprise that the overall use of temporary help is on an upswing.

HOW THE USE OF TEMPORARY WORKERS IS CHANGING

We've witnessed an increase in the number of companies using temporary help as a method of prescreening potential permanent employees. What better way to "test" a person's work habits, talents, ethics, and attitudes than to have them actually working for you? The large number of temporary workers who've ended up with permanent jobs gives credence to this phenomenon.

Another change in the use of temporary workers is the level at which they function. The clichéd perception of temporary help has been that of warehouse workers and inventory clerks. Although companies continue to seek men and women to fill these jobs on a temporary basis, they're also making better use of highly educated and trained people to assume managerial positions on a temporary basis.

On any given day, more than a million temporary employees are at work in U.S. industry. According to figures released in April, 1992, by the National Association of Temporary Services (NATS), this workforce is comprised of

- 63 percent office support workers
- 22 percent professional workers, including doctors, lawyers, engineers, accountants, managers, technical workers, and drafters
- 15 percent industrial workers, including custodians, stock handlers, shipping and receiving clerks, and truckers

The increase in the use of temporary *professional* workers is most striking. To meet the growing demand for temporary workers with advanced education and business skills, Robert Half International's temporary assignment division, Accountemps, provides executive temporary personnel for such jobs as controller, chief financial officer, and management information systems (MIS) and data processing manager. Many of these highly qualified individuals are hired on a permanent basis once the companies see what they have to offer as they fulfill their temporary assignments.

Skilled temporary help can be instrumental in building the morale of permanent employees. Permanent staff members have a lot more confidence in the security of their jobs when management handles normal fluctuation in staffing needs with the use of temporary workers, as opposed to a constant cycle of hirings and firings. In the parlance of the '90s, it's called "rightsizing."

The crucial need to train tomorrow's employees to handle increasingly complex office technology will place considerable strain on every company. It will also have a significant impact on the temporary employment business. According to a report published by *Business Week* in September, 1988, as many as 50 million workers will require training or retraining in the 1990s to stay in step with changing technology. It appears to me they were right. The cost of providing such training to permanent employees has been estimated by the American Society of Training & Development to range between $6,000 and $25,000, depending on skills required. For a company to bring in, on a temporary basis, workers already possessing these needed skills can result in significant savings.

This explosion in the need for technical training touches every industry and profession. It was reported in the October 1989 issue of *Personnel Magazine* that high-tech temporaries are increasing at a rate of between 300 and 500 percent a year. The *Magazine* also reports that professionals will be the fastest growing segment of the temporary services industry in the 1990s. The temporary employment industry has done a good job of keeping pace with these changing needs. New temporary firms that focus on narrow-niche specialties crop up every day. The trend is clear.

Who are these educated and experienced workers who choose to work on a temporary basis? They generally fall into one of three categories:

- Individuals who want to test several companies and positions before committing
- People who turn to temporary work because of the flexibility it offers, and as a means to better balance home and work life
- People actively seeking full-time jobs, who use temporary work to generate needed income during their unemployment

No matter what temporary workers' motivations might be, they should be prepared to step in and begin immediately. To have to train temporary workers beyond the expected initial orientation is to negate the advantage of hiring them in the first place.

USING TEMPS AS A STAFFING STRATEGY

The *planned* use of temporary workers as an important component of flexible staffing is important and should not be relegated only to filling holes when aspects of the overall staffing plan fall short. When companies integrate temporary workers into their staffing plans from the beginning, their long-range staffing goals are met more efficiently and with fewer surprises.

The first step in the planning process is to analyze each department from the viewpoint of task functions, rather than from the traditional approach of "one person, one job." Some tasks will naturally demand full-time, permanent employees, but others will not. Certain jobs will peak at predictable times and slacken off at others. Having someone on the payroll full-time to handle the peaks, but to sit idle during slower periods, isn't cost-effective.

When an employee resigns and leaves, the usual reaction is to seek a replacement immediately. This is based on the assumption that because the job had been handled by a full-time employee, it's necessary to hire another. It's possible that another person or two in the department can absorb the work the departed employee had been doing. If so, a raise for the few remaining workers who take on the added responsibility is considerably less than the cost of hiring another person. It also boosts morale and productivity. If the workload becomes too heavy at times, the use of temporary workers to augment permanent employees will level the load, at less yearly cost to the employer.

Following are general guidelines any company can use to determine how best to benefit from a flexible staffing philosophy.

Carefully Analyze and Reevaluate Job Descriptions

While most job descriptions contain a variety of duties, the usual approach is to hire applicants who meet the *highest* skill level required for the job. In reality, a person may use that highest skill level as little as 20 percent of the time. This results not only in wasted compensation, but also in the possible creation of a situation in which an employee becomes bored by the lesser demands of the position and loses the motivation to achieve top performance.

Examples of this type of situation might include

- Information systems staff capable of designing new systems, but who actually spend most of their time doing software upgrade installations.

- Accounting professionals capable of financial modeling and analyses, but who spend the bulk of their time performing tasks more appropriate for a full-charge bookkeeper.
- Customer-service telephone specialists who are equipped to respond to the most difficult customer requests, but who deal with a few routine questions on 80 percent of calls.

In the first two examples, the higher-level work is relatively "turn-key," based on special skills rather than specific company training and knowledge. In these cases, the company might reduce the skill level required for the permanent jobs and supplement with specialized temporaries who possess the higher skills. They would be utilized only at the frequency needed to accomplish goals.

In the third example, the higher-level work requires solid knowledge of the company, its products, and its policies. In this case, the company might establish two levels of telephone service, with 80 percent of routine calls answered by a combination of a lower-skilled, permanent staff supplemented by specialized temporaries. The other 20 percent would be routed to a small core of permanent staff members possessing higher skill levels and knowledge of the company.

Identify Flexible Staffing Areas

An analysis of task functions by job is the best way to accomplish this. There may be several "red flags," however, within an organization that can lead to some suitable targets. These include the next three categories.

Positions with fluctuating workloads. The accounting department is an obvious example, with its roller-coaster schedules of tax returns and year-end closings. Most companies have volume fluctuations in other areas, too, such as the following:

- Order processing follows sales cycles which are seldom evenly distributed.
- Data entry parallels the increases and decreases in direct-marketing activities.
- Information systems conversions must take place in the shortest possible time to maintain departmental productivity.

Positions with a heavy use of overtime. In most organizations, a certain amount of overtime is inevitable, but when the situation becomes chronic, one of two factors are likely at play:

- The position is truly understaffed.
- The position is staffed correctly from a time-allocation stand-point, but employee skills do not match the demands of the job.

Positions with high turnover or heavy absenteeism. These are often the product of staffing at a skill level that is substantially higher than what the positions actually require.

BUDGETING FOR USING AND HIRING TEMPS

Effective flexible staffing may prompt the need to budget for it well in advance. Human resources managers can play a critical role in helping line managers learn to build specialized temporaries into their ongoing budgets.

I've talked about the number of temporary workers who end up being hired on a permanent basis, and how some companies use the hiring of temporary workers as a testing ground for future permanent workers.

Keep in mind that top-notch temporary workers are the most valuable asset of the services that send them. While it's usually a joyous day for temporary workers when they land permanent jobs, the service that provided them is losing a valuable worker. Some services bill the hiring company a "conversion fee" based on a flat rate or other for-mula. Also, some services have clauses in their contracts stating that a temporary worker cannot be hired permanently until a period of 90-days following completion of the temporary assignment has passed. In either case, you should be clear about the policy before engaging a temporary worker, in order to be fair to all concerned.

What steps should a company take to utilize temporary employees most efficiently, and how can staffing professionals bring about a greater company-wide receptivity to the planned utilization of them?

A temporary worker is paid only for the time worked, which can translate into cost savings of as much as 20 to 35 percent, according to the U.S. Bureau of Labor statistics. This applies only if they have been hired correctly in the first instance and if their days on the job are structured properly. The resulting savings can be used effectively to boost morale for the smaller corps of permanent employees through raises and bonuses.

Choose the Right Temporary Service

Getting the most out of temporary help starts with having chosen the right temporary service, its experience, employee pool, and professional judgment and whether it is compatible with a company's general and specific needs. A correct match of job to temporary employee is critical. When selecting a temporary service, the following guidelines should be observed:

- Assign the responsibility for selecting the service to someone who knows how temporary help functions.

- Consider only services that are operated in a professional manner, by pleasant people who demonstrate respect for the workers they send on assignments.

- Determine costs in advance, and be specific. Some temporary employment firms charge a fixed rate, depending on skills required and the particular demands of the job. Some offer free training time on a company's equipment. Even the most skilled temporary worker may not be familiar with a company's configuration of computers, telemarketing systems, and other technical equipment.

- Don't hire a temporary solely on the basis of low cost. Efficiency, productivity, and cost savings are all key benefits of using temporary professionals. When arranging for a temporary worker, a common mistake is to look for the lowest rate. This can cost a company more in the long run because a less skilled person may take far longer to complete a task than would a more qualified individual.

For example, a worker who, at a rate of $10 per hour, takes ten hours to complete a project costs a company $100; a worker with more advanced skills who, at a rate of $15 per hour, takes six hours to complete the same project costs the company $90. In addition, this more skilled individual brings a greater degree of competence, innovation, and experience to the assignment and requires less initial orientation and ongoing supervision. This is simple arithmetic perhaps, but it is the sort of analysis that should not be overlooked when deciding what level of temporary worker to use. Find out more about the temporary service by exploring the following topics:

- Ask the temporary service to assign one account executive to work with the company. This person will become familiar with the company and its way of doing business, its unique culture, and its expectations of all employees, permanent and temporary. This can save time when a succession of temporary workers are hired, especially over an extended period.

- Find out if the service has enough skilled, experienced people available to fulfill a client's needs. Its pool of skilled temporary workers should be large enough to avoid having to send less qualified people when demand has depleted their ranks of the most capable. It doesn't cost the company any more to have a large enough temporary pool to complete projects quickly.

- Inquire about the temporary service's liability insurance, workers compensation, fidelity bonds, and errors-and-omissions insurance. The top services routinely provide them.

- Ascertain what recourse the company has if a temporary worker is not satisfactory. Will the service waive any fees? The best ones will, but with certain restrictions. For instance, any dissatisfaction might have to be reported to the service within a specified time (in some instances, within four hours of the worker having started the job).

- Purchase only the capacity and performance actually needed. Most of us follow this guideline when buying a product (such as a computer, a car, or a refrigerator), and the same holds true when buying the services of temporary help. If the job to be done has been accurately assessed, and the skills of the person to do it realistically evaluated, the right level of temporary employee can be chosen. (The same holds true when seeking a permanent employee through a personnel services firm. Keep in mind the right person cannot be identified if the task has not been carefully and accurately defined, and its parameters clearly communicated.)

USING TEMPORARY WORKERS TO STAY COMPETITIVE

There are as many solutions to staffing problems as there are problems themselves. What works for one company will not be applicable to another. However, with the goal of all businesses in the decades ahead being to remain competitive while keeping an eye on personnel costs, its utilization of skilled temporary and part-time help will play a predictable and increasingly crucial role.

Temporary employees are clearly permanent fixtures on the staffing scene, and are increasingly becoming a cost-effective, competitive staffing tool. Permanent staff appreciates their assistance, which certainly aids in their retention.

9

FORM BEFORE FUNCTION

Preparing Effective Job Applications

"An application blank should not be blank."

In many companies, job application forms are casually created and then assigned minor status in the hiring process. They're considered a necessary, but not terribly important, sheet of paper on which job applicants record routine information: Name, address, phone number, a few lines for previous employment data, colleges attended, name of the closest living relative, and maybe a section in which to indicate why they've chosen to seek employment at this particular company. When all the blanks are filled in, the application is filed away, perhaps never again to be seen.

To take such a backhand approach to creating and using application forms is to deny current realities. There are two basic reasons to put some care into these forms:

1. To create a document that will help employers gain as much insight as is possible into each prospective employee
2. To ensure that the forms do not violate the myriad employment laws presently on the books

USE JOB APPLICATIONS TO LEARN MORE ABOUT JOB CANDIDATES

From the aforementioned list, the first reason exists because, in part, employers tend to consider an applicant's resume as containing more relevant information than an application form, which is strictly "for the record." This attitude denies the fact that candidates have plenty of time to prepare their resumes. Words can be carefully chosen to put the candidate in the best possible light. Descriptions of jobs previously held are written, and rewritten, to make candidates sound, in too many cases, more important than they actually were.

Being asked to fill out a job application, generally on the spot, allows for little pondering or shaping. If the form's questions have been carefully considered by the employer, the candidates' more spontaneous answers can prove telling when compared to their resumes. An inconsistency between application and resume should become the basis for conversation during subsequent interviews.

Within reason, the more detailed a job application, the more can be learned about an applicant. This additional knowledge can pave the way for more meaningful interviews, or to preclude the need for an interview at all.

There are some job candidates who either refuse to fill out the application, or purposely or accidentally overlook some of the questions. If the job seeker refuses to conform, in almost all cases you'd be wise not to proceed with interviewing. The exception would be if you already have that information from other sources such as a friend who recommended the applicant. Even then be wary because applications require a signature indicating that the facts stated are true.

ADAPT JOB APPLICATIONS TO DIFFERENT JOBS

One of the basic problems with most job applications is that they're designed and printed—and rarely changed. I would counsel job candidates to create different versions of their resumes to apply to different job possibilities and to customize each covering letter they write. Why doesn't that apply, as well, to employers? In this age of computers and word processors, the task of customizing any document is easy and quick.

The entire application doesn't have to be redone each time a job opening exists, but an additional sheet of questions, prepared by the human resources department after consultation with the manager for whom the person will work directly, can certainly become part of the application filled out by all candidates for that particular job. Here are some examples:

- "What level of active participation and interplay with colleagues was expected of you in your previous employment?"
- "When under pressure on the job, what steps do you take to alleviate the pressure and to get the job done?"
- "What are the most important attributes you feel you can offer an employer?"

The short space allocated for an answer to each of these hypothetical questions demands brevity and specificity. At the same time, it gives the employer a tangible indication of whether the candidate can, indeed, communicate, at least in written form. Description of previous responsibilities on a resume can be crafted over a period of time, perhaps even shaped by a friend or family member proficient with the written word. No such person is present, however, when an application is filled out.

The use of an extended, made-to-order job application has a natural relationship with employment testing, which is good. A company that values written communications skills, and considers them necessary in a given job, should be prepared to test whether candidates possess them. If that can be accomplished as part of the job application, so much the better.

MAKE SURE JOB APPLICATIONS COMPLY WITH HUMAN RESOURCES LAW

The second reason for paying attention to job applications is a strictly legal one. We hear a great deal about interview questions that cannot be asked of job applicants. But the application is often the first direct contact between prospective employee and employer, and, it results in a written document. If the questions asked are illegal, no matter how subtle, it's there in writing for all to see.

How recently has your company's standard job application form been reviewed by legal counsel? If it has been more than a year, it's time for a fresh look.

What an application can or cannot contain depends, to a large extent, on the laws of the state in which the company does business. In general, there are certain basic questions that should be left off, if only to practice a better-safe-than-sorry approach. Here are some examples of areas to avoid:

- Questions pertaining to whether the applicant is a United States citizen can lead to trouble if asked on the application, or verbally, prior to hiring an individual. You can, however, inform applicants that they may have to prove their citizenship if hired.

- Questions that deal with marital status or number of children should be omitted.

- Questions about a woman's plans to start a family can, and have, been the basis for successful sex discrimination suits.

A careful and ongoing analysis of employment law, along with equally careful scrutiny of all company written material—including job application forms—should become a regular ritual, a cost of doing business. While the lawyers are taking a look, management, in concert with the human resources department, should be deciding whether current application forms need revision in order to make them more useful to the hiring process.

10

READING BETWEEN THE LINES

Reviewing and Evaluating Resumes

"Some resumes are unimpressive because the candidates who wrote them told the truth."

The first step in evaluating a resume is to determine whether it's fiction or nonfiction, autobiography or novel. Robert Half International surveys indicate that approximately 30 percent of job seekers lie on their resumes—and this doesn't include lies of omission! Knowing this, how do employers and human resources professionals know who's telling the truth and who isn't? Of course, the right kind of interview, in which questions raised by the resume are explored, coupled with a thorough check of references will often answer this question. On the other hand, sometimes it won't.

I really can't proceed with a chapter on resumes without reference to my monthly column, "Resumania," which has appeared in Dow Jones' *National Business Employment Weekly* since 1984. Of the millions of words written on the subject of landing jobs and building careers, the majority have focused on how to prepare an effective resume. Countless job seekers continue to ignore all this good advice, and concoct resumes that end up in the "Resumania" files. Some are so blatantly ridiculous that any prospective employer to whom they're sent can only laugh and look for the trash basket (in which to file them). Some are sent to me for use in "Resumania." I've collected thousands of them over the past 20 years. Here are just a few:

- "ACHIEVEMENTS: Flunked the CPA exam with high grades."
- "GEOGRAPHICAL RESTRICTIONS: Will not accept employment in foreign countries, including New York and California."
- "STRENGTHS: Acuracy in all phases of my work."

Even relatively straightforward resumes often fail to accomplish what they're supposed to do—generate an interview.

A resume will never ensure a job for a candidate (nor should it; employers who make a hiring decision based substantially on what may be fictitious information have better odds of success at a Las Vegas roulette wheel). At the same time, a poorly prepared resume will lose plenty of job opportunities for what may have been an excellent candidate.

A good resume should provide a hiring authority with nuts-and-bolts information about a candidate's education, experience, work history, and perhaps a modicum of less pertinent, more personal data. It can also, however, depending on the diligence and experience of the person reading it, give more subtle, but no less important, insights into its author's personality, motivation, seriousness about job and career goals, written communications skills, sense of order, and other revealing, albeit intangible, information.

DON'T RELY ON RESUMES TO ACCURATELY REPRESENT AN APPLICANT

For job candidates and employers alike, resumes are pretty much considered a necessary evil. Human resource professionals know they can't take resumes at face value, which makes their job harder. Job candidates realize that no matter how hard they toil at creating The Great American Resume, it might not portray them favorably enough to guarantee finalist status, especially when the competition is keen for a great job at a great company. Wanting to reach that stage probably accounts, to some extent, for the tendency to overstate accomplishments and responsibilities on resumes. I've heard some candidates say, "If my resume gets me an interview, that's all that matters. Once I'm there, I'll sell myself and worry about references later."

Before delving into what an employer should look for on a resume, and what lurks between the lines, it's important to view job seekers as basically falling into one of three groups.

- First, there are those who come off a lot better on paper than in-person. They won't get a job because of their excellent resumes, but they won't lose one either, unless they have inadequate interview techniques which trip them up.

- The second group comprises individuals at the opposite end of the spectrum from the first group. They shine in-person, but you'd never know it from their resumes, which are poorly written, inconsistent, disorganized, filled with superfluous material, and, in general, just plain wrong. It's always sad to run across such candidates. They often are the perfect people for jobs being offered, but they are never considered because of their poorly prepared resumes.

  Of course, in many cases, their inept resumes say something important about their approach to work. If they won't take the time and effort required to create a good resume, one can't help but wonder whether they are as cavalier when on the job.

- The third group consists of individuals whose resumes accurately reflect their education, work experience, accomplishments, and goals. It is within this category that you will probably locate Mr. or Ms. Right.

The resultant problem is that with so many exaggerations of candidate capability, employers are naturally skeptical of *all* resumes. I urge anyone charged with evaluating resumes to assume that what is contained in them represents the truth, until, of course, subsequent interviews and reference checks prove otherwise.

CUTTING THROUGH RESUME HYPE

It should be remembered that every resume is necessarily self-serving, so for a job candidate to deliberately understate credentials and accomplishments would be silly, at best. A resume is the candidate's sales brochure, advertisement, commercial. There should be a certain element of "sell," as long as it doesn't cross over the line into misstatement. A strongly worded claim of past achievements isn't necessarily dishonest, provided the facts wrapped up in the words reflect the truth.

If a resume is viewed as a job candidate's "ad," common sense can be applied when evaluating it, just as is done with other types of advertising. For most people, skeptical antennae go up when an advertiser makes claims that don't ring true. "The best!" "The most popular!" "The least expensive!"—buzzwords that cause speculation regarding whether there are facts to back up these proclamations.

Resumes often contain their own buzzwords:

"Knowledge of . . ."
"Exposure to . . ."
"Investigated . . ."
"Reviewed . . ."
"Examined . . ."
"Studied . . ."

These and other vague phrases promise considerably more than they invariably deliver. None indicate that a candidate has had direct involvement with or knows very much about the subject to which the phrase is attached. For example, *studied* can mean either an intensive curriculum in a subject or a one-night, high school adult-education course; *knowledge of* can refer either to having read a book or to having worked extensively with the subject in a previous job. These buzzwords should cause anyone reading them to make a note that will prompt probing those areas should the candidate be brought in for an interview.

To stay with the advertising analogy, it is known that many advertisers use loud music and announcers to draw attention away from the competition. Many job seekers seem to feel a similar need when preparing their resumes, which may arrive printed on hot pink paper, wrapped in bows, some with a photograph of the candidate, others running a dozen pages and even longer. I've seen resumes with blaring headlines on poster-size paper.

"HIRE ME AND YOU HIRE THE BEST!"
"LOOKING FOR THE PERFECT PERSON? HERE I AM!"

Such off-beat approaches usually garner attention, but they seldom result in a positive response. Other more mundane, black-on-white, carefully worded resumes seem dull by comparison, but it's the "dull" resume that usually represents that rarity of resume writing—the truth.

BE WARY OF FUNCTIONAL RESUMES

Just as there are three basic types of resume writers, there are two basic formats for resumes, chronological and functional.

The *chronological* resume essentially lists previous employment in order of the dates they occurred, with the most current listed first, and the earliest ones last. In contrast, the *functional* resume mostly ignores dates of employment. This type generally is used by people who have been out of the workplace for a period of time, who want to change careers, or who are attempting to cover up a job-jumping record.

Although more difficult to analyze than a chronological resume, a functional resume has its use. A woman who left the workplace in order to raise her children, and later wishes to re-enter it, will not have an employment history from which to create a chronological resume. Instead, she will focus on skills from previous employment, as well as continuing education and skills development during her years away from the workplace. In this case, a functional resume is perfectly acceptable, but one submitted by a person who has worked during recent years should raise eyebrows.

CONSIDER THE APPLICANT'S "JOB OBJECTIVE" CAREFULLY

When Robert Half International counsels people looking for jobs, we suggest they leave "Job Objective" off their resumes. I've seen it work against a candidate countless times. For example, a good candidate lists a narrow job objective such as "software sales." The company receiving the resume has chosen another candidate to fill the sales position, but a job opened up the day before in the software training department. The candidate who'd been rejected for the filled sales job has the right background to fill the training slot. Unless the human resources person looks beyond the stated objective—and many will not—this otherwise qualified candidate's resume will be discarded.

For a candidate who does include "Job Objective" on a resume, it's worth reading for clues to the person's aspirations. Are they realistic? Are they strictly self-serving or indicative of an interest in a growth-and-learning opportunity? Is there a sense that such candidates recognize that their objectives must meld with those of a company?

My "Resumania" files bulge with examples of job seekers who've used "Objective" to limit their options. One even stated: "OBJEC-TIVE—A pleasant job paying enough to support my loving family including six adorable kids. One dog. Two cats. One canary."

The job objective isn't the only thing to be left off a resume. There is no reason for any candidate to indicate why they left previous jobs. That's better reserved for the interview. One thing to look for, however, if such information has been offered, is the tone in which it's presented. A bitterness toward a former employer should be considered in a negative light.

PAY ATTENTION TO NON–WORK-RELATED INFORMATION

Most resumes contain a section in which the candidate indicates interests and hobbies, a section overused on too many occasions. Unless a hobby or extracurricular interest coincides with that of a potential employer or bears upon the job being sought, there's little to be gained by including it. Of course, there are things that can be learned by studying a job seeker's hobbies and avocations. If the list is long, it raises questions about whether this person will have enough time left over to devote to work.

Resume writers who dwell on irrelevant material might be attempting to cover up their own professional inadequacies. Some go to the extent of virtually obliterating pertinent information. At Robert Half International, we have seen resumes from men that list all children by name and birthdate and include the wife's maiden name and ancestral lineage. One resume highlighted a job seeker's wife's professional credentials to the point that she appeared a more attractive candidate than her husband.

Some skillful resume writers, without much to offer in the way of solid experience, focus on the name-recognition value of companies for whom they've worked, rather than on their functions and responsibilities. The effort sounds good on paper, at least during a cursory read, but if the candidate's words are analyzed, the lack of substance becomes apparent.

WHAT TO LOOK FOR IN A RESUME

Until this juncture, the emphasis has been on the negative aspects of resumes—those things that should raise red flags. In addition, here are positive attributes to look for in a resume:

- Tangible accomplishments that contributed to a previous employer's bottom line.
- Tangible attributes the job candidate can bring to a new employer that will enhance its bottom line.

The ideal candidate should be:

- *Interested.* The candidate should be interested in learning the job and growing within the company, rather than in obtaining instant gratification and reward.

- *Profit-oriented.* Does past work experience demonstrate how the candidate contributed to cost savings and increased profits? If not, why not? A good candidate might have failed to indicate such information on the resume. If so, it can be explored during interviews. If a resume already reflects it, however, you're that much further along in making a reasoned evaluation.

- *A team player.* An excessive use of "I" rather than "we" can tell volumes about a candidate. Good managers are comfortable sharing the glory. In fact, they go out of their way to give credit to others.

- *Ethical and loyal.* Does the resume bad-mouth previous employers or hint that the candidate will bring to the new job trade secrets learned while at a previous employer? If the latter is present, chances are good that the same thing will be done to you when the candidate seeks greener pastures.

- *Serious.* Flippancy, cuteness, and humor do not belong on a resume nor in an accompanying letter.

- *Organized.* Nothing indicates a sense of organization better than a well-written document. If the resume is disorganized, the writer probably is, too.

- *Comfortable in communicating.* Is the resume well written? Does it state what the writer intended without ambiguity? Are spelling and punctuation correct?

- *Ambitious.* Does the resume address itself to your company and the job you wish to fill? Or is it a cookie-cutter resume intended to appeal to all, regardless of the specific demands of the job being sought? Similarly, has the accompanying letter been written to a specific individual in the company, as opposed to the to-whom-it-may-concern variety? A truly ambitious candidate will take the time to individualize resumes and correspondence to fit specific needs.

- *Detail-oriented.* Job seekers who pour themselves into their resumes and who write different versions to match individual opportunities reveal their levels of energy and commitment.

- *Knowledgeable about the job he or she is pursuing.* Again, an individual approach makes this point. A good resume will be directed at the job and company. Those portions of the candidate's background that are directly applicable to the job and firm will have been highlighted and given priority.

TIPS FOR READING RESUMES

Here are some additional thoughts on evaluating resumes.

- Keep in mind that resumes that emphasize "Education" are appropriate for recent college graduates only. Job seekers who have been in the workplace for awhile should have pertinent work experience to highlight. Undue emphasis on education can mean a lack of actual work experience.

- Read from back to front, bottom to top. People tend to put the most unfavorable material at the end.

- When confronted with a functional resume, be especially alert to the possibility of long gaps between jobs.

- Beware of candidates whose list of memberships in business and civic groups is unusually long. Joining groups is easy to do. The question is what have they contributed to those groups. Relevance is key, too. I knew one candidate who listed membership in six airline frequent-flyer clubs.

- Look for a straight and positive career path. Does it demonstrate consistent growth and the ability and desire to take on new challenges? Did previous employers recognize such contributions and reward them accordingly through promotions to greater responsibility?

- Be wary if the resume is long on generalities and short on specifics. Specifics shed light on *real* work history and accomplishments. "Descriptions" often add up to nothing more than puffery.

- Make sure claims of managerial responsibility make sense when viewed against the job held. A middle-level manager purporting to have supervised hundreds of people, and an inordinately high budget, is probably exaggerating. Skillful interviewing and careful reference checks will determine whether the suspicion is justified.

11

TURNING THE ONE-ON-ONE INTO A WIN/WIN

Interviewing Effectively

"Intuition is not a good substitute for logic."

An effective interview involves preparation, careful execution, and follow-up. As axiomatic as that may sound, many employment interviewers fail to pay attention to all three elements.

Some of us are more naturally comfortable interviewing people than are others. For example, successful radio and television talk show hosts bring to the task a natural ability to probe and to listen. They enjoy a good conversation and know how to keep it going. Most importantly, they're skilled in eliciting answers to the questions *they* want answered.

Good employment interviewers don't need the same level of skills as Oprah, Phil, or Larry King. Employment interviewing techniques can be mastered by anyone who realizes that it is a learned skill.

A good employment interview represents the proverbial two-way street. Thoroughly prepared ("right") questions are asked and the answers are properly followed up and evaluated.

Note that I haven't talked about "right" answers. Too many job seekers know all the right answers. What I prefer to emphasize are the sort of responses that enable interviewers to make reasoned decisions about a candidate.

PREPARING FOR THE INTERVIEW

Job seekers are constantly reminded in books and magazine articles to come prepared for an interview, but there is considerably less written emphasis placed on the need for *employers* to prepare. There are undoubtedly good reasons for this, including an unstated attitude that a person seeking a job has more at stake than the company offering it.

The defense I often hear from managers who shortcut the interviewing task is that they simply don't have time to "do it by the book." Usually, these busy executives sandwich in interviews only after other business has been addressed. In too many cases, they depend on their human resource professionals or their assistants to handle the interviews and recommend finalists. Although I recognize that today's executives must accomplish more with fewer people, I urge that they assume responsibility for interviewing job candidates, and that it be elevated on their list of priorities.

Too often, interviews begin with the interviewer pulling out a resume and saying, "Okay, let's see what this says." This not only fails to uncover potential problems with candidates, it short-changes them; they're deprived of thoughtful questions to lead them into fruitful areas of discussion.

Many people are uncomfortable questioning another person's veracity and consequently back away from asking tough questions. Most important to them is that the atmosphere remain free from confrontation. Experienced interviewers have learned to handle sticky questions without injecting unpleasantness into the conversation. Job candidates submit resumes as their calling cards. The information contained on them is purported to be accurate. Any employer has the right, as well as the obligation, to determine just how accurate the information really is.

At the same time, a candidate's resume should urge interviewers into areas that allow, even encourage, candidates to exhibit why they're right for the job. The proper questions can go a long way toward accomplishing this.

The following sections cover interview questions that have proved effective over the years. They are divided into three basic categories:

- Job-related skills and experience
- Intelligence and aptitude
- Personality and attitude

Before asking candidates any of these questions, there's one statement that should be made early in the interview: "Please answer my questions any way you wish, but also think about how your former superiors and employers will answer the same questions about you."

This delivers a subtle (albeit clear) message that references will be checked.

Asking About Job-Related Skills and Experience

Question: "Please describe a typical day on your present (last) job."

The candidate is prompted to go beyond the simple description of responsibilities and duties that appear on the resume. Since the interviewer knows what's expected of a person filling the job, with this question he or she can ascertain whether each candidate typically functions in a manner that closely approximates those needs.

Question: "Tell me about the people you hired in your last job. How long did they stay with you, and how did the ones you hired work out?"

The answer to this can give a solid indication of each candidate's ability to assemble and retain a staff. Be alert to hints that the candidate had trouble keeping employees for an appropriate duration, or may have had other deficiencies in leadership skills.

Question: "What would you say is your single most noteworthy achievement or contribution in your present (or former) job?"

Most resumes give a general indication of accomplishments. The candidate who can substantiate the resume's claims with details should rank high in an interviewer's estimation. Don't immediately rule out a candidate who stumbles over this question. Job applicants often have contributed far more than even they are aware.

Question: "Tell me, how would you install a standard cost-accounting system [or any other procedure that relates to the position you're trying to fill]?"

Or, *"If you ran into this situation [present a typical problem with which the candidate might be expected to deal as your employee], how would you handle it?"*

Presenting a hypothetical question can be an excellent way to test a candidate's know-how and can establish a candidate's candor. An individual who attempts to bluff through such questions won't be as impressive as one who admits the need to gather more information and to give it more thought before attempting to resolve it.

Question: "What do you think it takes for a person to be successful in [fill in the specialty]?"

This encourages candidates to reveal strengths and weaknesses. Candidates will invariably cite what they perceive to be their individual strengths. Attributes they fail to include could indicate those they lack.

Question: "What specific strengths do you think you can bring to this position?"

Ask this before having revealed details of the job to be filled. If candidates are told what the job demands before you ask this question, they may feel it necessary to tailor their answers accordingly.

Determining General Intelligence and Aptitude

Question: How do you make important decisions?"

Does the candidate seek out others for information and advice? Is he or she action-oriented or analytical? Look for evidence that each candidate has actually made important decisions in prior jobs. When faced with making such decisions, did the approach taken represent an open, flexible mind or a need to follow a rigid set of rules?

Question: "What are some things your present employer (or former employer) could do to be more successful?"

This question is double-edged. First, the answers indicate whether the job seeker sees improvement as an overall challenge or prefers to deal with smaller, narrowly focused approaches. Second, it can serve to uncover a negative attitude toward former employers. If the answer is a litany of complaints, it represents an attitude that could prove counterproductive to a company's morale and team spirit.

Question: "What do you know about our company?"

What candidates actually know is less important than how hard they've worked to ferret out information. Individuals who've expended time and energy to learn about prospective employers demonstrate initiative and commitment to success.

Assessing Attitudes and Personality

Question: "Why are you interested in this job?"

The objective of this question is to separate candidates who are looking for any job from those who are genuinely interested in the company. Candidates who fall into the former category are those who often send out form letters (To Whom It May Concern, or Dear Sir) and who use a catch-all resume instead of tailoring versions to specific job openings.

This question can also help establish whether a candidate's career ambitions mesh with what the job and company can realistically offer.

Question: "Why have you decided to leave your present position?"

Taken at face value, this question often reveals what motivates a candidate, for example, money, career growth, or personal challenge. In most instances it's all three, but one much more than the others. Be prepared to ask follow-up questions. If the reply is, "My boss and I butted heads all the time," ask why. In what areas did conflict seem most often to emerge? What attempts were made to alleviate the situation? Had it happened before with other superiors?

Personality conflicts can and do happen with even the best of people and shouldn't automatically disqualify a candidate, nor should having been fired. It's a matter of discovering the *reasons* for a dismissal and evaluating a candidate's overall candor.

Question: "What would you like to be earning two years from now?"

Does the reply reflect a realistic perception of the candidates' worth in the marketplace? Do the candidates' career and income goals mesh with what the company wishes to provide?

Question: "What have been the biggest failures or frustrations in your business life? What are your major weaknesses?"

Replies can indicate how well candidates know themselves, as well as how comfortable they are about revealing weaknesses. This question often brings about a clichéd response: "Not having enough time to accomplish everything I want to accomplish," or "I expect too much from myself." As with all such general answers, ask for specific examples.

Question: "What risks did you take in your last few jobs, and what was the result of having taken those risks?"

Studies indicate that people who take calculated risks are generally more successful than those who avoid risk. Some candidates will shy away from admitting having taken risks in previous jobs. Other less "calculating" candidates will *risk* acknowledging having taken some. In either case, follow up. Why hadn't they taken risks? If they had, probe the factors they considered before taking them and whether the outcomes were successful.

Question: "Is there something you consider a failure in your professional life, and if so, why do you think it occurred?"

What's sought here are signs that candidates willingly accept responsibility for something that went wrong. Astute job prospects know that most interviewers are wary of people who blame others for their shortcomings, so for interview purposes they will take blame for a minor incident. You may want to probe further by asking pertinent questions such as, "To what extent do you feel responsible for the loss of earnings at your last company?"

SITUATIONAL INTERVIEWING

The questions in the previous section represent a "traditional" approach to employment interviewing and focus on candidates' resumes, employer job requirements, and the use of hypothetical situations and subjective self-evaluation. If handled correctly, and if the interviewer follows up on responses, a substantively revealing portrait of a candidate can be drawn.

There is yet another candidate dimension that, if known to a prospective employer, can prove useful when choosing from a field of relatively equal candidates. This is each candidate's actual job skills.

Human resource specialists estimate that as little as five percent of the information obtained in a standard interview pertains to skills actually required for a job. Experienced job seekers have honed responses to such traditional interview questions as, "Where do you see yourself five years from now?" or "What are your strengths and weaknesses?"

The traditional employment interview results in little information about candidates' "real-time" skills—how they might handle multiple work assignments, long working hours, tight client deadlines, and a variety of other job-related skills.

To help correct this, a new interviewing technique has been developed within the past decade. Termed *situational interviewing*, or *behavior description interviewing*, it's based on the premise that the best indicator of future behavior is past behavior. Additionally, it's designed to obtain maximum information about past behavior as it relates to specific job-related skills. (The same tactics used with candidates during situational interviewing can be employed when talking with reference givers about candidates' skills and background.)

The questions used in a behavior description interview are developed through a multistep process that begins with the collection of observed job-related behaviors, or "critical incidents." A critical incident is a past event or behavior that defines successful job performance in specific terms. Such incidents can be generated through face-to-face interviews with a candidate.

Learning about critical incidents requires more prompting than traditional interviewing usually entails. People tend to describe their own behavior, or the behavior of others, in general terms. For example, when asked to describe the behavior of an effective staff member, an initial response is likely to be subjective and nonspecific: A manager might refer to a former employee as "hard-working, technically competent, and good with customers." A job candidate, when asked to offer strengths, often gives the same brand of subjective answer. Vague phrases, however, do not offer critical incidents; no specific event or past behavior has been described.

To be useful, critical incidents must describe *actual behaviors and events* experienced by the candidate or observed by a superior or peer. For example, if prompted to describe specifically how she is "good with clients," a candidate could recount the time a client of the accounting firm for whom she'd worked lost inventory data in the process of converting to a new computer system. The candidate stayed late a few nights and provided the missing information, using data from prior years' documents. The client wrote a letter of appreciation to the candidate's manager, a copy of which is in her personnel file.

This is a critical incident. It defines a specific situation in which the candidate exhibited initiative and *proved* that she is "good with clients."

Step One: Defining Effective Job Skills

The more critical incidents generated, the better. One candidate might highlight a series of incidents in which she was faced with multiple tasks and deadlines. Her approach was to prioritize each task and to complete them based on this analysis. Obviously, this is an organized individual with the ability to inject order into potential chaos.

Another candidate might point to a succession of times when it was necessary to devote virtually full-time to the job, including nights and weekends. In each instance, he arranged for his family to visit relatives in order to work unimpeded. He not only is willing to expend extra effort when called on, he and his family also have what appears to be a solid, mutually cooperative attitude, certainly a plus if the job being filled will demand such extra effort.

Still another candidate recalls critical incidents involving the need to work in close concert with people from other departments. The skill? The obvious ability to put together a team and to be an effective contributor to it.

Step Two: Developing Effective Interview Questions

If the job has been clearly and accurately defined, behavioral or situational interviewing can be more narrowly focused to directly link response to job. For instance, if a keenly developed organizational sense is deemed to be an important requisite, the behavioral questions can be tailored to that need. "Tell me about a situation at work or in school where you were under pressure to complete multiple tasks simultaneously. How did you handle that situation?"

Other questions designed to elicit critical incidents applicable to a specific job might be as follows—I call them "tell me" questions:

Objective. Ability to plan tasks.

Questions:

"Tell me about a big project you had to plan for school or work."

"What was the project?"

"What steps were involved?"

"What was the outcome?"

Objective. Ability to prioritize.

Questions:

"Tell me about a situation in which you had several things to do in a limited amount of time."

"What led to the situation?"

"How did you handle it?"

"What was the outcome?"

Objective. Ability to delegate.

Questions:

"Tell me about a time when you were in charge of a project and had to enlist the help of others."

"What were the circumstances?"

"How did you assign the work?"

"What happened?"

Objective. Ability to handle customer relations.

Questions:

"Tell me about a situation in which you had to deal with customers."

"Who was involved?"

"What did you do?"

"How did they respond?"

Objective. Ability to be a team player.

Questions:

"Tell me about a time you helped resolve a group problem."

"What caused the problem?"

"What did you do?"

"How was it resolved?"

Objective. Ability to deal with personnel at all levels.

Questions:

"Tell me about a time when you had to work closely with someone in a position above (or below) you."

"Who was the person?"

"What did you have to do?"

"What was the outcome?"

Objective. Ability to problem solve.

Questions:

"Tell me about the most difficult job or school problem you've ever had to solve."

"What was the problem?"

"What steps did you take to tackle it?"

"What were the results of your efforts?"

Objective. Ability to apply knowledge.

Questions:

"Tell me about a situation in which you had to apply some newly acquired knowledge or skill."

"What was that knowledge or skill?"

"What led to the situation?"

"What were the results?"

Objective. Ability to know limitations.

Questions:

"Tell me about a time when you needed outside help and had to ask someone for assistance."

"What was the situation?"

"Who did you ask for help?"

"What was the outcome?"

Objective. Ability to take initiative.

Questions:

"Tell me about a time when you had to take charge and start the ball rolling to get a job done."

"What were the ramifications if the job didn't get done?"

"What did you do?"

"How did it turn out?"

Objective. Ability to learn on the job.

Questions:

"Tell me about a time when you had to learn something new in a short amount of time."

"What created that situation?"

"What did you have to learn?"

"How did you learn it?"

"What was the result?"

Objective. Ability to communicate.

Questions:

"Tell me about a time when someone misunderstood something you had said or written."

"What had you said or written?"

"How did you make yourself clear?"

"What was the outcome?"

Objective. Ability to listen.

Questions:

"Sometimes people listen but don't hear. Tell me about a time when you misunderstood a teacher or superior."

"Why do you think you misunderstood?"

"How did you resolve the misunderstanding?"

Objective. Ability for commitment to work.

Questions:

"Tell me about a time when you had to finish a job even though everyone else had given up."

"What was the situation that led up to it?"

"How did you manage to finish the job?"

"What was the final result?"

Objective. Ability for commitment to service.

Questions:

"Tell me about work you've done in your community or in a school organization."

"What did you contribute to the cause?"

"How did you balance your time between work and this community activity?"

"What was the outcome?"

The actual questions can be as varied as the interviewers asking them. The important thing is not to settle for general statements. The five standard questions used by journalists—who? what? why? when? where?—definitely have applicability to employment interviewing.

Step Three: Conducting the Interview

A situational interview is not intended to be a replacement for the more traditional format, nor should it be considered separate and apart from it. Properly utilized, it renders the traditional interview *more* effective.

Questions of a general nature based on a candidate's resume are important, of course, just as the information and "feelings" gained through an applicant's demeanor, social skills, and interaction with an interviewer can be telling. By incorporating elements of the situational approach into the traditional interview, useful information about job-related skills can be gleaned that might not otherwise be obtainable.

As any experienced interviewer will attest, it's difficult to handle silence on the other side of the desk. Obviously, any candidate should have the right to reflect when confronted with an unexpected, nontraditional question. Interviewers often find it difficult to refrain from stepping in too quickly while a candidate stops to think. Some applicants will find it difficult to think of specific examples, and others will ramble. It's incumbent on the interviewer to take control and to channel the responses into a more concise format.

Other responsibilities of the interviewer include

- Not spending too much time on any one question
- Not allowing the applicant to change the subject
- Not "leading" the candidate. Sometimes, interviewees offer an incident that reveals more about them as people or their suitability for the job than they intend. When this occurs, interviewers should remain neutral and not overreact. Expressing surprise or negativity, whether through words or facial expressions, can undermine the interview and prompt applicants to change their responses.

- Not accepting incidents at face value. Occasionally, an applicant's response is so strongly positive or negative that a misleading picture emerges. Faced with this, an interviewer should attempt to obtain contrary data to provide a more balanced picture. For example, if a candidate volunteers information that school or company rules were broken to accomplish an objective, the interviewer might ask about a time when the candidate obeyed the rules even though it meant goals would not be achieved.

GENERAL INTERVIEWING TECHNIQUES

Conducting an effective employment interview, whether traditional, situational, or the desired combination of both, involves a number of disciplines. Like every aspect of the hiring process, a good interview doesn't "just happen." It evolves out of attention to detail and to certain time-tested techniques:

- When possible, phrase questions indirectly and off-handedly. For instance, "If you really think about it, what would you say are your greatest strengths?" is better than "What are your strengths?"

- Give candidates ample time to respond to questions. Thoughtful silence does not mean indecision.

- Link new questions to past answers. Consider this example: "We've established that you enjoy taking on responsibility. Can you think of some good examples of when and how you did?"

- Be nonthreatening when seeking more elaborate answers to a question. Comments such as, "That's interesting," and "Could you tell me more about that?" are less threatening than "What do you mean by that?" "Maybe you could clarify that point for me" is less intimidating than a curt "Why?"

- Balance questions to avoid dwelling on negatives. Grilling a candidates early in the interview only puts them on guard, making it more difficult to elicit candid responses as the interview progresses. If candidates continually dodge an issue, be certain the issue is germane to the job being filled before pressing for an answer.

- Pay attention to the applicant. Most employment interviews take place in an office, but some don't, either by design or because circumstances dictate a different milieu. No matter where interviews take place, however, every candidate deserves the interviewer's undivided attention.

- Don't pressure the candidate. There are some interviewers, although they are in the minority, who believe in establishing a pressure atmosphere to rattle candidates. That approach generally proves counterproductive. More useful information is obtained in a relaxed setting, be it the interviewer's office, a conference room, a hotel lobby, an airplane, or a restaurant.

- Try using offbeat "tests." Over the years, I've experienced a generous offering of not-so-traditional interviewing techniques. One of our good clients liked to place a book on the floor between the door and the desk. Candidates couldn't miss it, and most stepped over it. The candidate who picked up the book and placed it on the desk was the one usually hired by this client.

- Don't ignore bizarre behavior. We've actually interviewed—but didn't hire—the following candidates, whose behavior was certainly unconventional.

  - One candidate unwrapped his lunch during an interview and ate it.

  - Another candidate broke into a tap dance when told she was seriously in the running for the job.

  - A gentleman had his beeper go off twice and asked to use the phone.

  - Another person threatened the interviewer if the job wasn't offered.

  - Several people fell asleep during their respective interviews.

  - A woman asked for the interviewer's astrological sign before allowing the interview to proceed.

There are some common mistakes sometimes made when interviewing candidates; here are tips for how to avoid making these mistakes:

- Don't forget to take adequate notes, to make sure you don't overlook the best candidate, usually one who was interviewed early in a long list of candidates. A fair and useful evaluation of each candidate can only occur if the interviewer has made careful notes. Psychotherapists follow a good organizational rule-of-thumb: 45-minute sessions, with the hour's remaining 15 minutes reserved for note making.

- Don't overlook what I consider to be a vitally important candidate characteristic—wanting the job. When faced with candidates of roughly equal attributes, choose the one who wants the job the most.

- Don't give interviewees answers to key questions. When an interviewer says to a candidate for an accounting position, "Budgets are very important in this job. Do you have a good background in budgets?", it's the rare applicant who would not answer, "Yes."

- Don't lose control of the interview. Savvy candidates know that they should attempt to gain control. If they try to move the interview in a direction other than what the interviewer wishes, the focus should be redirected and more probing questions should be asked.

- Don't ignore testing candidates' communications skills. One way is to ask for an explanation of technical jargon they used when answering a question.

- Don't fail to notice candidates' lack of enthusiasm, particularly about current employment. Measure the level of job interest by asking, "What excites you most about your job?" or, "Tell me something about your company's best customer."

- Don't pre-hire. Too often, candidates are hired before they even sit down. They look right (usually similar in "type" to the interviewer), and their resumes read right. It pays for an interviewer to step back in these situations and to challenge candidates to "prove" they are right for the job. Interviewers who are prone to hiring stereotypes should do more prescreening over the telephone.

- Don't ask departing employees to participate in interviewing their replacements. This is almost always a mistake.

CONDUCTING TELEPHONE INTERVIEWS

If done properly, one-on-one, face-to-face interviews consume considerable amounts of time. In our current business climate where more must be accomplished with less, time is truly of the essence. This undoubtedly accounts for an increasing use of the telephone for prescreening applicants. Using the telephone for employment interviewing creates its own particular set of guidelines.

- Be certain candidates can speak freely. This will seldom be the case if prospective employees are called at their current place of employment. If nothing else, it sets up a tension that's calculated to get in the way of a productive conversation. Instead, arrange to speak with candidates at their homes, or suggest they call you from a public phone when out of the office.

- Treat telephone interviews as though they were being conducted face to face. Top radio personalities compensate for the inability to see their listeners by imagining a person sitting on the other side of the microphone and speaking to that person, rather than to an unseen audience.

- Limit distractions as you would when conducting a face-to-face interview. Have your other calls held and bar visitors to your office until the interview is completed.

- Don't conduct a telephone interview in place of a face-to-face interview; the phone interview does not preclude the need to meet in person. But it can weed out candidates whose answers to preliminary questions are inadequate or whose verbal communications skills are sub-par.

CONCLUDING THE INTERVIEW

Ending an interview is usually the hardest part. Some interviewers have so much trouble with this that their interviews end up being considerably longer than they need to be.

Failing to officially end an interview can result in considerable confusion. Witness what happened to an executive at one of the largest companies in the United States: He failed to end an interview with a prospective employee in such a way that the interviewee understood. The executive left the office. Four hours later, a secretary found the candidate still sitting in the room waiting for the interviewer to return.

If an interviewer with the authority to hire and to set salary and benefits parameters feels the perfect candidate is sitting across the desk (subject to thorough reference checking, of course), it should be made known to the candidate. If a candidate looks that good to one interviewer and company, chances are he or she will look as good to others. If the candidate isn't almost "locked up," the company risks losing that individual, perhaps to an important competitor.

If certain candidates seem right but the interviewer wishes to look further, these candidates can be told, "I think you are an excellent prospect for this position, but I want to give you a chance to think it over. Call me in a couple of days and let me know if you are definitely interested."

For candidates whose interviews rule them out of consideration, they should be informed as quickly as possible so they don't count on getting the job.

It has long been my contention that interviewing, just as every other phase of hiring, should be codified to the extent possible. At the same time, I recognize that employment interviewing is as much an art as it will ever be a science. From my perspective, "perfect" employment interviewers are people who have learned and assimilated the rules of effective interviewing, and then have proceeded to practice them in their own inimitable styles.

12

TESTING ONE, TWO, THREE . . .

Giving Applicants Pre-employment Tests

"It's foolish to think tests are foolproof."

Before it was fashionable to sue at the drop of the proverbial hat, the only real question about pre-employment testing was whether it resulted in the hiring of better people. That question still exists, but because testing now plays a integral role in numerous employment-related lawsuits, a large second question emerges: Is it worth the risk, even if it does result in better hires?

The answer depends on many factors, the two most salient being the nature of candidate being tested and hired, and the care with which the test has been prepared.

MAKE SURE TESTS ARE LEGAL

A candidate applying for any job requiring a specific skill—typing, shorthand, filing complex documents, or other knowledge of something tangible and precise—can be tested effectively with virtually no risk of litigation. I stress the word *virtually*. For instance, if a typing test is one of two such tests, one harder than the other to disqualify otherwise equal job candidates, you may be vulnerable to lawsuit.

Although skill tests will always be of value, just how useful are the myriad psychological and personality tests that are routinely administered by companies? In too many cases, non–skill-related testing is used to compensate for an inadequate hiring process. Because the choice of a new employee is substantially subjective, using test scores provides a comfort level for some employers.

The problem is that even the finest of psychological and personality tests fall short of accurately predicting an individual's future success. There are usually too many intangible factors that go into individual performance to be identified through formal testing for higher-level positions.

A risk any company runs when injecting employment testing into its hiring decision occurs when the test is devised by outsiders and without adequate legal review. *HR Professional* has created what it terms a *privacy audit*, which is reproduced in Exhibit 12-1. The statements in the audit are applicable to a variety of privacy matters. If all, or nearly all, of the statements are answered "True," the test is basically non-invasive and probably acceptable. If only a few items are checked as true, it's best to reconsider its use and resulting selection procedure.

CONSIDER APPLICANTS' REACTIONS TO TESTS

The legality of testing aside, public perception should also be considered. Unions fervently fight random drug testing of their membership. Polygraphs, once popular in the arsenal of pre-employment testing, are now illegal in most situations.

In the summer of 1990, the University of Missouri–St. Louis released the results of its survey of 197 Employment Management Association members. The survey was intended to gain a better understanding of the respondents' perceptions of pre-employment testing. Respondents rated drug testing, genetic screening, and polygraph exams as the most offensive forms of pre-employment testing. The least offensive were unstructured interviews, targeted interviews, reference checks, and accomplishment tests. Work samples, personality tests, honesty tests, weighted application forms, and medical exams were judged as falling somewhere between.

I believe that astute candidates can safely "fudge" their answers to personality tests to suit the job they are seeking. For example, if a person were applying for a position in sales, he could answer questions to indicate he has an outgoing personality. If, on the other hand, a candidate were seeking a job in computer programming, she could

Exhibit 12-1.   Privacy Audit for Testing Job Applicants

1. Test items are job relevant.
2. Random and unannounced testing is avoided.
3. Relatively inoffensive test items are used.
4. Applicants sign an informed consent agreement.
5. Test scores are kept confidential.
6. Access to test scores is on a need-to-know basis.
7. Test scores never become public for any reason.
8. Test booklets (used and unused) and scoring keys are locked up at all times.
9. Applicants understand the business necessity of the testing program.
10. Applicants are treated with respect and courtesy.
11. Only properly trained staff administer and use the test.
12. Only legally permissible items are included in the test.
13. The test complies with relevant professional and legal standards.
14. The test is fair to protected subgroups of the population.
15. The test has been sufficiently validated.
16. The test is the most accurate selection procedure available.
17. Test administration guidelines are followed consistently.
18. The test is accurately scored.
19. The test is one part of an overall selection process.
20. Test givers are trained to protect applicants' privacy rights.
21. Written guidelines on test security and data protection are followed consistently.
22. Test scores are not included in automated corporate data bases.
23. Applicants are not adversely "branded" or "labeled" based on their test scores.
24. The employment test is used only for purposes for which it was designed and validated.
25. When requested, applicants can receive feedback on their results.

answer questions to indicate that she has a very conservative personality.

From a legal perspective, *non-invasive* is the operative word when deciding whether a pre-employment test is valid. But your belief in the worth of testing itself should determine whether your company includes it in its employment practices.

13

SEARCHING FOR THE TRUTH

Checking References

"A bad reference is as hard to find as a good employee."

Of all the steps in choosing a person to fill a critical position, none is as important as checking references. Despite the inherent problems associated with that task, it can be done, and done to the extent that it helps a company make reasoned hiring decisions.

Be aware that a company can be held liable if it *doesn't* check references. A major company was sued for its failure to adequately check the references of an employee who committed rape while in its employ, and who had previously spent time in jail for that same offense. This was considered "negligent hiring." Another court may come up with a different opinion.

Reference checking in the 1990s has become a mine field. Companies are sued for giving references, for giving "inaccurate" references, or for simply giving references with which job candidates aren't happy. The result is that many companies will do nothing but confirm dates of employment when asked for a reference. This opens the door for certain "creative" job seekers who know that "disinformation" on their resumes is likely to go undetected.

The process of reference checking should begin at the time of the candidate's interview. As suggested in Chapter 12, start with, "Please let me know if your references would answer any of the questions we discuss today differently, and if so why that might be. If we're interested in you, and you're interested in us, we'll be checking your references. By the way, please feel free to check our references as well."

Take good notes during the interview. If there's a difference between what a reference and a candidate have said, it can be raised with the reference.

As with every aspect of hiring, the procedures a company uses to check references should be subject to legal review before being implemented. Following are some general guidelines to keep in mind:

- Obtain candidates' approval, in writing, to check references.
- Have printed on all application materials a veracity statement to the effect that if candidates misrepresent facts and are hired, they will be subject to dismissal. (The wording of the statement should be reviewed by legal counsel.)
- Ask candidates to give permission, in writing, to their most important references that they have the candidates' permission to be completely candid.

HOW TO OBTAIN CANDID REFERENCES

Ironically, according to a 1993 study Robert Half International commissioned, employers who *expect* an honest reference said they hesitate to *give* one. At the same time, the higher up reference-givers are on a company's organizational chart, the more likely they are to give candid references—an important finding when determining whom to seek out when checking references.

The respondents in this study were queried about the relative merits of attempting to obtain references through different methods:

- Written references from former employers were judged to be the least reliable. Only 37 percent of respondents (top management and personnel management) expected those who wrote to be candid. When the same people were asked if *they* would be candid when giving a written reference, only 26 percent answered affirmatively. It's obvious that managers at all levels are reluctant to commit their statements to paper, especially if a reference is less than positive.
- References given over the phone were perceived to be more reliable than those in writing: Fifty-one percent expected a candid

reference when seeking it over the phone; 46 percent replied that they would give an honest and open telephone reference.

- Obtaining references through personal visits produces the most reliable information. (This confirms what I've advocated for many years.) Of the respondents, 70 percent expected candor on a personal visit, with 56 percent saying they would also be candid in a face-to-face conversation.

- The question of whether friends give, and expect to receive, honest references produced its own set of numbers: 67 percent of all respondents expected a high level of candor from a friend, but when respondents were asked, "Would you be more candid if the person contacting you was a friend?," only 54 percent said they would be.

- Finally, the study investigated whether top managers or personnel directors are more candid. It became clear that, overall, top management offered considerably more information than did Personnel—whether the reference was in writing, over the phone, in person, or from a friend.

With this in mind, the method for obtaining references and the level at which to obtain them dictate the following respective actions:

- Make personal visits.
- Seek references at the highest possible management level.

No matter how thorough reference checks may be, there will always be those who come up with their own individual and, at times, skewed analysis of the results. The president of a $50 million manufacturing company once told me, "The better the reference, the more anxious the company is to get rid of the employee."

I asked the obvious question: "Does that mean if a reference is bad, the candidate is good?" His response was, "No." He went on to say, "Chances are that any good references are because they're afraid of lawsuits."

Operating under that philosophy, checking references is a waste of time. Except that it isn't!

WHO SHOULD CHECK REFERENCES?

In our aforementioned study, 87 percent of executives surveyed agreed that if the employee about to be hired is to work directly for them, they should personally check at least one of the candidate's references (72 percent agreed strongly; 15 percent agreed somewhat). Whether these same executives follow through on what they say should be done is conjecture. It has always been my contention that managers to whom new employees will report should personally check as many references as possible, at least the ones with the most pertinent information to offer vis-à-vis the job being filled.

I know, I know: Who has time to do that? That's what a human resources department is for.

Although Human Resources can and should handle a considerable amount of reference checking, it should also restrict itself to checking the basics: verification of previous employment and education dates, criminal records, job title, nature of job, and, if possible, salary and responsibilities. Also, discrimination laws apply to reference checking the same as they do to interviewing. A company cannot probe into marital status, age, handicaps, religion, race, ethnic background, or national origin for the purpose of using such information in a hiring decision.

Even when Human Resources obtains the basic "facts," these references do not uncover the more intangible, albeit important aspects of a candidate's ability to perform: attitude, hands-on experience, ability to function as a team player, people and communications skills, and numerous other factors that should be known before making a hiring decision. This information must be checked by the hiring manager.

WHO TO CONTACT

First, check the obvious, those references the candidate has supplied. Ask for as many references from the candidate as possible. Then, consider those at the bottom of the list as the most important. They may well be the ones who will be most candid if a candidate has put the least flattering individuals last and hopes you will give up before calling the entire list.

For harried executives anxious to fill positions, references provided by the candidate (called "canned" references) are often considered "good enough." Individuals on the list are called and say nice things about the candidate.

Candidate-supplied letters shouldn't be totally ignored. Here's why:

- When calling someone who has provided a candidate with a written reference (the letter provided by the candidate should not be mentioned), you can determine whether statements made in the letter conflict with what the reference has to say. Like questionable entries on a resume, this forms a basis for further questioning.

- If a candidate is hired, and problems with performance soon surface, a "disinformation" letter can be used to mitigate possible legal action should it be necessary to dismiss the new employee. Employers who write glowing letters about undeserving former employees can land in legal trouble. If the letter attests to a former employee's honesty and then that same person embezzles funds from a new company, and it's further discovered that the employee embezzled from the company that had given the reference, this may well be grounds for a lawsuit against the former employer.

After contacting the references the candidate has provided, contact the candidate's immediate supervisor, or the person above the immediate supervisor. These are the people who should be most familiar with the candidate's day-to-day work.

Contact your counterpart at the candidate's current company. When president speaks to president, controller to controller, MIS manager to MIS manager, more candid and detailed responses are likely. The person who does the same work you do at the company providing the reference is most likely to level with you.

Network. Ask reference-givers to supply the names of other persons to contact.

Personal references, including friends, relatives, teachers, and clergy, generally have limited value in reference checking, but contact them, too. They sometimes offer a unique insight, and can lead to still other sources.

Tap into your own network, even if the employee has never worked directly for people in it. Friends, or friends of friends, may know of the candidate or of someone at the candidate's company who has not been considered as a reference. Sometimes, competitors of the company for whom the candidate has worked can supply helpful information, particularly if the candidate has high visibility within an industry.

WHAT TO ASK WHEN YOU CALL FOR A REFERENCE

Once it's time to check references of candidates who are deemed to be seriously in the running for the job, planning how to approach it is extremely important. Everyone's time is at stake—yours, as well as the people providing the reference. The prospective employer should focus only on those candidates who stand an excellent chance of being hired, provided their references check out. (Candidates should be judicious when providing references, limiting their use for the job opportunities they really want and stand a good chance of obtaining.)

Because so many executives are reluctant to give references (legal considerations aside, it takes time), the approach taken by an employer is important. Before contacting a reference, attempt to find out something about the person in order to establish something in common— a hobby, sports or theater interest, town of residence, school, or business. One way to accomplish this is to ask the candidate during the interview to tell you something about former bosses and other potential references. Obtaining such information is not intended to turn a reference call into a prolonged, unfocused conversation. Rather, it is because being asked to provide a reference often sets up a defensive posture. Anything to put the reference provider at ease can help establish a more open, candid atmosphere.

Once you've made contact with a reference-giver, a statement such as the following can set a proper stage: "I want to be fair with Ms. Brown and be sure she's the right fit for our company. I'd appreciate it if you would help me, and Ms. Brown, by being candid."

Here are some questions you might initially ask that deal with basic facts about the candidate, in this case our hypothetical Ms. Brown. They are easy to answer and don't apply pressure because they don't ask for opinions. (They can be asked even if the human resources department has already asked them.)

1. "I'd like to verify her dates of employment. I understand she worked for you from September 1990 until last month."
2. "What were her responsibilities?" "What was her title?"
3. "I'd appreciate knowing her salary when she left." "Did that include bonus? Overtime? Incentives?"
4. "For whom had she worked prior to joining your company?"

Once these simple, innocuous questions have been asked and answered, more difficult issues can be raised:

1. "Do you consider Ms. Brown to be honest?"
2. "How does she compare to the employee who's currently doing

the job?" Or, "What characteristics will you look for in the employee to replace her?"

3. "You seem to think very highly of her. I'd be interested in knowing why, if she was that good, you didn't try to induce her to say? Have you tried to rehire her?"

4. "How did she perform under pressure? The job we're considering her for involves tight deadlines."

5. "Since none of us is perfect, or succeed at everything we do, what are some of Ms. Brown's shortcomings?"

6. "Have you had an opportunity to see Ms. Brown's current resume? Let me read you the part that describes her job with your company." (Stop at each significant point to allow the reference to comment.)

7. "Not all employees like everyone with whom they work. How did she get along with her colleagues?" (If a problem with another employee is indicated, follow up with, "What factors led to the problem with that person?")

8. "Was she dependable, that is, did she arrive on time, stay late when necessary, take minimal sick days?"

9. "How did Ms. Brown come to work for you? Was she referred to you by someone?" (This is to determine whether she was hired based on the recommendation of a personal friend, relative, customer, or client.)

10. "What did her references say about her when you hired her?" "Who actually checked them?"

A reference-checker must evaluate the answers to these and other questions in terms of the *perceived* honesty, candor, and sincerity of the reference-giver. An experienced interviewer has the ability to glean information from tone of voice, hesitation, and other intangible factors.

Some executives are better at the art of conveying ambiguity than are others. I once knew a man who called a company to check the reference of its former employee. He asked the company president to tell him something about this person. The president responded, "He worked for us for 20 years and we were satisfied when he left."

Some executives, aware that someone is calling to seek a reference for a former employee, become masters of evasiveness. They avoid such conversations by being unavailable for the calls. When faced with such stonewalling tactics, many employers seeking references give up. This is unfortunate, as well as unfair to both the company and candidate. There is a natural suspicion that sets in when a former employer refuses to provide a reference. Why? Is something being hidden? Does the former employer know it can't honestly give a favorable reference, yet wish to avoid potential legal action by the former employee? The candidate faces losing out on a good job because of such suspicions. The company loses out on hiring a top-notch person.

One way to proceed when faced with such a situation is to write the reference a letter similar to the one in Exhibit 13-1.

The message is subtle, yet clear. By not responding, Mr. Smith could be held responsible, legally and morally, for a good person's losing an important job opportunity. The key in this strategy is to send a copy of the letter to John Jones. Hopefully, he'll contact Mr. Smith and urge him to accept your call.

DOUBLE-CHECK NEGATIVE REFERENCES

Bosses are sometimes so angry when good employees leave, they'll go out of their way to give a bad reference. If a reference hints at being

---

**Exhibit 13-1. Sample Letter
Requesting a Reference**

Dear Mr. Smith:

I have been attempting to reach you in connection with a reference for Mr. John Jones, who had been in your employ.

We are considering Mr. Jones along with two other people for an important position with our company. Since we consider his work record with your firm to be highly significant, we cannot consider him further unless we speak to you.

I'll call you again in a few days in the event you don't get around to calling me.

vindictive, and the candidate appears to be right for the job, raise the points made during the negative reference with subsequent references, or go back to those already checked. It is hoped that this will more than balance the single negative remark. It takes a lot of hard work to counteract a bad reference, but when it happens, a company can gain an excellent employee who, because someone has deliberately interfered with his or her chances, has had difficulty landing a good job.

There is always the possibility, of course, that the negative reference was deserved and that subsequent reference checks will confirm this. That's why careful digging with additional references is necessary.

Personality conflicts between former employers and employees also can "color" a reference. When a reference checker suspects this situation might exist, it's time to check the reference's references.

Call other people with whom you've already spoken at the same company and have established a good rapport to ask whether they know of a problem between the former employee and the reference. It can be put this way: "You might remember I called the other day to check Helen Gray's references. There's a small point I hope you can help me clarify. I checked with Joe Green, who wasn't especially complimentary about Helen. All her other references have been fine. Any idea why Mr. Green might feel this way about her?"

One of two things will happen. Either Joe Green simply didn't get along with Helen Gray and is attempting to harm her career, or there's a certain amount of truth in what he had to say about her performance. Either way, you'll have drawn a more accurate picture of her as a candidate.

EVALUATING REFERENCES

Once references have been gathered, the next step is to accurately evaluate them. Objectivity is paramount. Neither longevity on a job nor promotions and raises necessarily indicates that an employee was more than merely adequate. We all know pleasant incompetents who are well liked, and who not only survive but also prosper at their companies.

In order to come up with a fair and useful evaluation of references, make contact with more than just one person. What sometimes happens is that the first reference extols the virtues of an individual without hesitation or reservation. The employer, anxious to fill the job, is lulled into false confidence and abandons further reference checks. This can lead to a serious hiring mistake.

The first and only reference may feel sorry for the personable but inept former employee and be willing to do almost anything to help that person land a job. On the other hand, the reference may be so anxious to rid the company of deadwood that giving a glowing but false reference is viewed as "good business." Because this happens more than we like to think, it has created that cynical theory mentioned earlier in this chapter that the better the reference, the more anxious the company to rid itself of the employee.

There is also the school of thought that if you can't find something wrong with a candidate, you haven't done a thorough job of checking references. I happen to subscribe to this philosophy.

Everyone has some weakness, some flaw. That is not to say that once uncovered, such flaws and weaknesses are grounds for ruling out the individual for employment. Far from it. However, until an employer touches base with a reference who indicates some negative factor, no matter how small or insignificant, the process shouldn't be considered complete.

Were the questions asked of references designed to elicit meaningful, useful answers or were they of the open-ended variety that encourages answers the reference seeker *wants* to hear, questions such as, "Do you think she can handle the job as treasurer for our company?" or, "Is he a hard worker? Is he loyal and honest?" These questions, and others like them, encourage only answers that are of little or no use to an employer. This can be avoided by applying the situational interviewing techniques outlined in Chapter 11. Although it isn't easy in the business climate of the 1990s to obtain specifics about a former employee's performance, it can be done if diligence and creativity are applied. If a cordial and trusting atmosphere has been established between reference-seeker and reference source, attempts to probe beyond generalities are often successful.

A comment such as, "His work was excellent," is fine, but what does it really mean? Perhaps the reference neglected to mention that the candidate was unable to complete complicated tasks.

"She's an accounting genius," certainly says something about the candidate, but that same person might also have been an abysmal failure when asked to manage people, an important factor to know if she's being considered for a managerial position with a new firm.

RE-CHECKING REFERENCES AFTER HIRING A CANDIDATE

Reference checking doesn't necessarily stop once someone has been hired. Suppose the final selection has been made and the new employee has been on the job for a month. His work has been good, but he has called in sick four times and has been late on five other mornings. Maybe it's just an unusual circumstance that does not constitute a pattern of behavior and will not be repeated in the future. It could also be a precursor of things to come.

Time for a renewed stab at reference checking. Get back to some of the same people who were cooperative during the initial round of checking and ask them something along these lines: "Remember me? You were good enough six weeks ago to give me a reference on Richard Park, who we hired. Everything is fine, but during the last four weeks he's been absent four times and late five. Did you encounter that problem when he worked for you?"

It is hoped that the answer will confirm that your new employee's behavior is an aberration and doesn't represent an ongoing problem. However, if he had established such a pattern with his previous employer, that knowledge better enables you to call him in for a frank talk. Let him know that some of his references have told you they experienced similar problems with him and that you will not tolerate a continuance of this behavior. The employee, faced with corroboration of your complaint, certainly can't defend his actions as unique. He'll either stop such behavior and become the sort of employee you'd hoped when hiring him, or you'll be forced to dismiss him. It is better that this unpleasant action happen early in his employment rather than later.

Checking references should be a priority in everyone's hiring procedures. The cost in time and money is small compared to the much larger cost of hiring the wrong people. No company can afford that.

14

DECISIONS, DECISIONS, DECISIONS

Choosing a Candidate

"A decision-maker isn't afraid of making the wrong decision."

Decision making comes naturally to most of us. For others it is a source of considerable grief. Everyone in a position to hire must eventually make a decision, which can be especially difficult when the candidate field is strong and more than one man or woman is clearly right for the job.

Choosing a good new employee can be especially difficult if the hiring authority has sought the "perfect candidate." No such creature exists. For those who insist on seeking perfection, jobs usually go unfilled for a very long time until reality wins out.

All hiring involves compromise. Trade-offs must be acknowledged. No candidate is without weakness, without flaw. Strength in one area might compensate for weakness in another. Certain gaps in knowledge and skills can be remedied.

Just as for most of life itself, there are no guarantees when hiring. Until individuals actually come to work and display their professional wares, they are unknown quantities no matter how impressive their resumes, their performance during interviews, and their references.

If all elements of the hiring process have been carefully considered and executed, the odds of making a mistake are minimized. If the process has been less pristine, the odds then increase that the wrong person could be chosen.

When two or more candidates are relatively equal, I have always advocated hiring the person who wants the job the most. No price can be assigned to enthusiasm and commitment. Individuals possessing these traits not only are more likely to give the job their all, they also stand a better chance of assimilating into a company's culture and remaining with that company for the long term.

Corporate culture, if allowed to play too pervasive a role in a hiring decision, can be counterproductive. Yes, we all want employees who "fit in," but not at the expense of fostering diversity of thought, philosophy, and style. Companies that clone former employees when hiring new ones eventually suffer from the sort of "inbreeding" that can prove crippling.

EVALUATING CANDIDATES

Although all hiring decisions must, of necessity, involve a certain level of instinct and intuition (personal "vibes"), four tangible factors are generally considered when evaluating candidates: experience, personality, intelligence, and education.

Experience

Experience is usually the most important factor for evaluation, but leaning too heavily on it with certain candidates can needlessly rule out other good people.

How important is it that experience must have been gained in the same industry in which the new company functions? John Sculley, chairman of Apple Computer, came from Pepsi. General Motors' chairman is John Smale, from Procter & Gamble. A friend of mine was turned down for a public relations job with a company that made and marketed peanut butter. The reason? Despite an impressive public relations background, she did not have "peanut butter experience."

How much experience in general is realistically required for a given job? Sometimes, people with the most listed experience are hired for the same reason as those who score highest on employment tests. It's safe to do so. If the new employee doesn't work out, those who did the hiring can point to test scores and lengthy experience to explain away the mistake—the mistake being that the new employee did not have the ability to do the job, when push came to shove, or did not have the willingness to do the work.

Certainly experience is important when determining who to hire. Recall the similarity to those critically important job descriptions mentioned earlier in the book. People who inflate the experience needed for a particular job cause more honest people to be rejected. As a result, the rejected candidates often end up lending their knowledge and skills to a more enlightened competitor merely because the company failed to adequately check references. If you are able to determine that the leading contender exaggerated the facts, the interviewer should reconsider and re-interview some of those who were rejected.

Judging candidates' relative experience should also take into consideration "trainability." A candidate with long and deep experience might not be as malleable as someone with less actual experience who would be open to a new way—your way—of doing things.

Intelligence vs. Education

It may sound axiomatic to state that intelligence and education are not synonymous. Still, countless employers assign undue credibility to certain institutions of higher learning and grade point averages from those institutions.

Like experience, just how much education does a person need to perform a specific job and to have growth potential? When should book knowledge give way to common sense ("street smarts")? What is the mix needed when choosing a person to fill a position? All things being equal, who wants the job most and for the right reasons?

Personality

Is a final hiring decision being swayed by the personalities of the competing candidates? A pleasing personality is always desirable. Is a candidate with better credentials and with more to offer a company in terms of skills, experience, and attitude being discounted because his or her personality isn't as scintillating as anothers?

The goal is to achieve a balance. Choose a person with too much education or experience and you may end up with a bored individual lacking a challenge. Place too much emphasis on personality and you may have someone who wilts when the real demands of the job must be faced.

AVOID COMMON HIRING MISTAKES

Every survey of the workplace Robert Half International has undertaken points to written and verbal communications skills as being the attribute most lacking in job candidates of the 1990s. Despite this, many of the same executives who reported said that they don't give it high priority when doing their own hiring. I think the reason is that the interviewer, in the final analysis, relies on hunches.

I almost always advise companies to avoid making the final hiring decision in a committee. The final choice between candidates should not be a committee decision. It's understandable to want others in a company to contribute observations and to participate in the hiring process, but if the number of decision-makers is large, a compromise candidate is the likely result. Hiring mistakes tend to compound in direct proportion to the number of people involved in the decision.

Here's a list of some additional "hiring traps." (There are many others, of course.)

- Cloning. Don't try to hire only those cast in your own image or in the image of the person who previously held the job.
- Irrational prejudices. One client told us, "Left-handed people are not as competent as right-handers." (He was left-handed.)
- Fear of success. "Will the person I hire replace me?" Good managers hire those who are capable of taking over.

WATCH OUT FOR RED FLAGS

So far, this chapter has focused on reasons *to* hire a candidate. There are also reasons not to hire someone.

The following list comprises what I feel are "signals," or "red flags," to a prospective employer; the person raising them should be scrutinized more closely. Each taken by itself might not be sufficient reason to rule out a candidate. Combine a few of them, however, and there should be serious doubts about the wisdom of hiring such an individual.

Be cautious when confronted with candidates who

- Leave a job without adequate notice.
- Accept the terms of an offer and then try to up the ante.
- Fail to be courteous to your receptionist, secretary, or assistant.
- Are late for more than one interview.
- Dress inappropriately.
- Can't point to specific work achievements.

- Didn't learn much about previous employers' business aside from their specific departments.
- Have no verifiable references, including employers who have died, are out of the country, or were with firms that have gone out of business.
- Have to travel far to work unless they're accustomed to doing so.
- Are truly over-qualified to the extent that boredom is likely.
- Are independently wealthy, unless they're up for the top job.
- Reveal confidential information about former employers.
- Are willing to violate a contract with a former employer.
- Lack enthusiasm.
- Have lied about material facts.
- Appear to be angry about prior employment.
- Didn't take the trouble to find out as much as possible about your company.
- Take too long to consider the offer.
- Bad-mouth former employers.

15

THE WINNING CANDIDATE

Making the Job Offer

"Procrastination is often the complication."

The decision has been made. All candidates in the running have done their best to sell themselves to the employer, and one has been chosen from the pack.

Once this stage has been reached, the prospective employer usually assumes the role of *buyer*. Who made the best sales pitch? Who "gets the order?" This sounds reasonable, except that the chosen candidate might not accept the offer.

It can be assumed that this individual represents the cream of the crop. Impeccable credentials. Solid references. The right experience, education, and skills. A person anyone—including other companies—would welcome on-board. Remember: The chosen candidate must be sold on the position and your company.

Sure, millions of people are happy to be offered a job and won't be fussy when it comes to the finer points; perhaps one may assume they are not outstanding candidates. Those who are—and there are plenty of them—will have employment options. Also, if, for some reason, they are in a difficult personal situation that prompts them to be less choosey this time around, they'll take the job but continue looking for something better. That's the revolving door.

BE CAREFUL WHAT YOU PROMISE A PROSPECTIVE EMPLOYEE

An employer has to be prudent, however, when selling a person on accepting the position. False claims and promises about a job and company are not only wrong when a salesperson makes them for a product or service, they can land a company in a courtroom.

An employee remembers an employer's promises, direct or implied. On the other hand, an employer may forget a promise to one of hundreds of people. Any offer made to a new employee, any promise of future promotions, raises, perks, and other inducements should be noted and carefully filed away. This is especially important when the person to whom a new employee will report promises things above and beyond standard company policy in order to bring the candidate on-board.

What's actually promised and what an employee perceives as having been promised are often quite different. For example, a prospective employee is told she'll be considered for a raise in three months. The employer means it only as a promise to consider a raise, but that candidate might hear, "You'll receive a raise in three months." That's why promises should be made crystal clear, both verbally and when noting them for the record.

HOW TO "SELL" THE COMPANY TO PROSPECTIVE EMPLOYEES

When a candidate is identified early as a strong contender, that's the time for an employer to begin selling. One way is to begin a process that bonds such individuals with the company and with those with whom they'll work. Introduce them to a selection of employees known to hold the company in high regard. Share a vision of the company's future plans with these candidates, at least to the extent that it does not compromise company security. It's hard to say no to something to which you feel you already belong.

An effective way to bond an attractive candidate to the company is for the manager to whom the person will report to share details of his or her own career growth. This establishes a mentor relationship of sorts; most career-minded candidates actively seek a mentor.

DON'T IGNORE OTHER CANDIDATES

If a candidate has accepted the job but has not, as yet, reported to work, the job hasn't been filled, which is why I advocate maintaining contact and a good relationships with the runners-up. If the winner decides, after all, to accept another offer, those candidates who came close to being hired should continue to be viewed as viable. If the first choice goes elsewhere, don't hesitate to get back to others who wanted the job and who possess the right credentials.

This can be taken a step further. Many candidates, when offered a job, respond with "I'd like some time to think it over." This is, of course, an acceptable response. How long should an applicant be given?

There's no set rule. Much depends on how badly and quickly the position needs to be filled, and other offers the candidate has received. The important thing is that *the employer* set the time.

During this period of candidate contemplation, an employer should continue to consider others for the position. Frankly, I believe that the search should continue—perhaps not actively but by keeping in touch with the runners-up—even after the winner has accepted the offer and until that individual actually begins work.

A prudent and savvy employer will keep those other people in mind, including their resumes, letters, and interview notes, until the new employee has been on the job a year or more, has demonstrated the qualities that led to being hired, and gives indication of being happy with the job and company.

For the same reason, I've always counseled job seekers who've been turned down for a position to keep in touch with the employer who hired someone else. Individuals decide at the last minute to accept another job that was slow in being offered, but one that they had preferred all along. In some cases they come to work for the new employer, receive the more coveted offer, and abruptly resign. In other cases, an employer realizes the company has made a mistake after a new employee has started work and finds it necessary to dismiss him or her.

In each of these scenarios, having knowledge of a few good people, by virtue of already having evaluated them through the hiring process, saves considerable time and effort.

HOW TO COUNTER A COUNTEROFFER

A significant number of job seekers receive a counteroffer from a current employer after they announce their decision to leave. Some seek a new job for precisely this reason—to have an edge when seeking promotions and raises. For others, whose performance has been exemplary, the current employer may sincerely wish them to stay and will sweeten the pot if they do so. Still others will confront their future employer with the counteroffer and use it in an attempt to gain a larger salary and increased benefits.

There's a certain aura of extortion when this latter scenario occurs, although many people are honest in reporting having received a counteroffer and are not using it to better their position. The salient point to remember when counteroffers enter the hiring picture is that in all but the rarest of cases, offering them or meeting them is foolish policy.

Statistically, people who receive counteroffers from current employers seldom last very long after accepting them. I estimate that as many as seven out of ten employees who accept a counteroffer are not with that same company one year later, either having quit because of the root discontent that led them to seek a new job in the first place, or having been fired because of being perceived as disloyal. A friend of mine, a career counselor, once personally tracked 43 men and women who'd sought his help. Each had received a counteroffer the last time they'd considered a job change. Of the 43, 31 decided to accept and stay at their current jobs. Within a little over a year, 28 of those had either been fired or had resigned. The other three were actively seeking new employment. When faced with a counteroffer from the company that currently employs the candidate you've chosen, point out to that person the statistical chances of his or her still being with that employer after a year.

There are job seekers who are not necessarily seeking more money by virtue of raising a counteroffer during hiring negotiations. Perhaps they are in need of extra confirmation of their worth to a new employer? Is there something that can be offered them that does not represent matching the counteroffer in dollars and cents?

An exceptionally good candidate placed by one of Robert Half International's offices reported having been given a counteroffer by her current boss. A little questioning revealed that she was seeking more money because of the cost of daycare for her two young children. Our client had not made much of his company's liberal policies toward flextime working arrangements. When this was highlighted and she had a fruitful discussion with our client that led to her being hired under such a flexible arrangement, the financial counteroffer was forgotten. This individual's need was care for her children. For someone else it could be a heightened sense of job security, assurances that the work will be challenging and that career growth is possible, or that working surroundings are pleasant and healthful. By analyzing such personal needs, the right buttons can be pushed to make the person perhaps realize, "That's really important to me. How can I turn this offer down?"

16

PUTTING IT IN WRITING

Using Employment Contracts

"A clear understanding is clearly an advantage."

Employment contracts are like prenuptial agreements. The underlying purpose is to anticipate problems that could arise should the relationship sour. In other words, in the event the "marriage" between the employer and employee fails, there could be a limit to costly surprises for both parties.

Generally speaking, an employment contract is more beneficial to the employee than to the employer, although it should be fair to both parties. Under terms of the contract, the employee is usually guaranteed a certain length of service or an agreed-upon amount of severance if the employer prematurely ends the employment relationship. To the employee it represents a form of job security, perhaps the only one left in this age of insecurity.

From the company's perspective, such a contract will probably prohibit the employee from using company assets, including customer lists and trade secrets, and working for a competitor for a prescribed period of time in an assigned geographical territory. Unfortunately, an employment contract cannot ensure hard work, dedication, and loyalty.

In this age of hyper-litigation, more employers are structuring employment contracts to better protect themselves from employee lawsuits. Previously, most employment contracts simply dealt with the terms of employer and employee parting ways, not with the *reasons* an employer might end the relationship. Because employers no longer have an ability to fire at will, once an employer's absolute right, the clearer the reasons in an employment contract for being able to dismiss an employee, the less the chance of a successful lawsuit after the fact.

WHAT TO INCLUDE IN AN EMPLOYMENT CONTRACT

Most employment contracts include an employee's job description, which can be valuable in the event it is necessary to dismiss the individual because of poor performance or the inability to perform required duties. This aspect of any employment contract should be worked out in concert with those who write job descriptions.

An employment contract should spell out the employee's compensation, including stock options, bonuses and profit sharing, and, if applicable, company cars, and other perks.

More than ever before, companies seek to control trade secrets. An employment contract should be written to include an enforceable confidentiality agreement. Its purpose is twofold. First, it puts employees on notice that if they misuse secret information, they will have breached the contract. Second, it serves as a psychological reminder to employees that should they disclose the company's trade secrets, they're likely to face legal action. When writing such an agreement, care must be taken to define, as specifically as possible, what constitutes "trade secrets" as they directly apply to the company.

ASK YOUR ATTORNEY TO REVIEW THE EMPLOYMENT CONTRACT

It is crucial that all of a company's legal documents, including basic employment contracts and confidentiality agreements, be drafted by a knowledgeable attorney. Legal counsel can and should play an even more important role than that of simply drafting agreements. By involving attorneys in a company's overall philosophy toward awarding employment contracts, a balanced, sensible approach can be taken. You and your attorney should consider the following issues:

- Are hiring contracts likely to enhance company morale or create an atmosphere of distrust?
- What overall impact do local laws have on hiring and firing, and will employment contracts help a company adhere to those laws?

- What is the judicial mood, locally and nationally, in regard to hiring law, and how will it affect the company's legal stance with employees?
- Who should receive such contracts?

Although most companies still reserve employment contracts for higher-level positions and eschew them for other employees (with the exception of when relocation is involved), the litigious society in which we all must function is gradually changing that. More people are seeking employment contracts before leaving one position for another. The extent to which any employers wish to cooperate depends on many factors. The salient one is how much a company wants to employ a particular person.

While no one can fault anyone for asking for an agreement with a new employer, the tendency to award them to a wider variety of employee strikes me as problematic. Like today's major-league, professional sports, in which it seems to me that players are more concerned with their security than with what they contribute to their teams, this movement in employment is at odds with an employer-employee "marriage" in which mutual growth and success should be the goal.

As with every other aspect of hiring, retaining, and, when necessary, firing employees, company policy and implementation of employment contracts cannot be taken lightly. Simply drawing up a "piece of paper" is not adequate to address the myriad issues raised by the concept of a written agreement between employer and employee. Employment contracts must be the result of prudent corporate thought, aided by enlightened and expert legal counsel.

PART II

KEEPING THE BEST EMPLOYEES

17

SLOWING DOWN THE REVOLVING DOOR

An Overview of Employee Retention

"A company's product or service, reputation and financial condition is predicated upon hiring and retaining the most qualified people."

In a perfect business world, turnover doesn't exist and the attrition rate is zero. Since a perfect business world exists only in theory, the reality is that employees come and go, especially in this age of increased career mobility and lessened job security. The goal is not perfection. It is to have as many good people *come* to work and as few of them *go* as is possible.

Some turnover is always necessary. If it weren't, every employee would eventually earn an excessively high salary. Death, sickness, relocation, retirement, and recruitment by other firms thin the herd, as it were, and ensure that there is always sufficient rotation of employees to prevent such an untenable, costly situation.

According to figures recently released by the Bureau of National Affairs, turnover averages 1.9 percent per month across all industries, or 23 percent per year. In some industries, percentages run higher, such as financial institutions at 30 percent and health care at 28 percent. In all cases, anything management can do to lower turnover rate is good for a company. The less that revolving door turns, the better.

THE EMPLOYER-EMPLOYEE RELATIONSHIP SHOULD BE A PARTNERSHIP

Subsequent chapters in Part II offer specific advice on motivating and retaining employees. For now, allow me a few general observations.

If ever an analogy was apt, it is that of a successful marriage. Finding a mate is not nearly as difficult as keeping that person, especially a mate of quality. It takes daily nurturing and attention, caring, and good deeds. When marrying, choosing the right person is a vitally important first step. The same holds true when hiring. Hire smart to begin with and the odds on keeping that person increase exponentially in your favor.

Recently, a friend told me about the company for which he has worked for many years. Because of the recessions and high unemployment rate, management dropped a number of programs that had been designed and implemented to boost employee morale and motivation. The reasons for dropping them weren't stated publicly, of course, but my friend learned why. Top management decided that because people are more afraid of losing their jobs these days, it no longer needed to spend money to keep them.

Ironically, and not at all surprisingly, some employees have left that company. Guess which? The better ones, of course—the very people the company will need most when things turn around and competition heats up. Employee retention is relatively easy—it's keeping the good ones that is difficult.

I enjoy using acronyms to codify ideas and to make them more readily remembered. Here's one that bears directly on retaining good employees—RETAINS.

- **R**espect all employees, at every level. Criticize them in private but praise them in public.

- **E**mpower talented employees who thirst for responsibility and who demonstrate readiness to take it on. Good people need challenges and the authority with which to meet them. They will make some wrong decisions, but a few bad decisions are ultimately better than being forbidden to make decisions at all. Deny reasonable empowerment to employees and they'll leave, usually at the worst time.

- **T**eams get more done than can individuals. Build teams and recognize team leaders and contributing players.

- **A**cknowledge outstanding performance by promoting from

within. Good people look elsewhere for recognition and promotion when outsiders are hired routinely to fill important jobs.

- Ideas and innovation are important to talented employees. Encourage creativity, even if it does not produce immediate tangible results. One day it will. Stifle people's creative output and they'll seek more receptive ears.
- Never say "never." Top performers soon wilt under constant negative responses.
- Salary and benefits must be competitive. Enhanced medical benefits, flexible working hours, assistance with daycare, and other "offerings" often are more important to a valuable employee than is an increased paycheck. Also, don't forget a pat on the back and a "Nice job" for good work.

DON'T NEGLECT YOUR EMPLOYEES

It's patently illogical for a company to devote precious time and money to the recruitment of the right person, only to lose that individual through neglect. Still, it happens every day.

The best people, the ones you've worked hardest to recruit, do not sever all connections with other potential employers by virtue of having accepted a job with your company. They keep their irons in the fire, and those fires generally stay hot. If a new employee arrives the first day feeling optimistic and fresh and leaves feeling abandoned and disillusioned, the lock on the revolving door has already been undone.

In general, here is a checklist of things for an employer to keep in mind when contemplating the subject of employee motivation and retention.

- Humanize the work environment.
- Avoid drastic overstaffing and understaffing.
- Spell out assignments.
- Delegate wherever possible.
- Encourage employee input.
- Publicize company goals.
- Promote from within.
- Set the proper example.
- Rotate job responsibility.

- Use a carrot, not a stick, to motivate.
- Put "stretch" into assignments.
- Establish reasonable deadlines.
- Be liberal with praise.
- Criticize with tact.
- Tell the truth.
- Say "no" tactfully, and only for good cause.
- Set up an effective incentive program.
- Don't take training programs for granted.
- Give individuals responsibility.
- Get rid of "bad apples" as quickly as possible.
- Don't whitewash unpleasant assignments.
- Take control of "time theft."
- Be aware of the signals of an unproductive working environment.
- Hold meetings only when necessary.
- Be consistent.
- Show a personal interest in the people who work for you.
- Learn from employees who quit.
- Admit mistakes.
- Share information with employees.

Many of these ideas are amplified in subsequent chapters.

RESPECT EMPLOYEES AND GIVE RECOGNITION TO GOOD WORK

Praise is better than a raise. Cynics scoff at the notion, but in my experience a lack of respect and recognition causes as much employee dissatisfaction as does insufficient compensation.

No misunderstandings here. We work to earn money. Then again, many rich people, who never have to work another day, toil harder than they did before coming into wealth. "One does not live by bread alone," applies to the majority of employees.

Salary and benefits must be competitive, of course, but there should be a parallel "payment" in the form of challenge, respect, and recognition. Most employees prefer to stay on their jobs. It doesn't matter what their reasons are. The natural tendency is to stay put. Failing to tap into this natural inclination by not making employees feel respected and valued and by not praising them for their accomplishments, is to risk losing them.

There's also a downside to the tendency of employees to wish to remain in their current jobs. This occurs when they stay only because of tangible benefits or because other jobs are hard to find. The result is lowered morale and reduced productivity.

According to a recent *New York Times/CBS* survey, three in ten Americans say they, or someone in their household, have stayed in a job they wanted to leave in order to keep their health benefits. This means that approximately 30 percent of those who responded to the survey are simply hanging on to a job, hardly the necessary ingredients for dedication, motivation, and productivity.

Offering a health care plan sufficient to retain employees should be viewed only as a building block. They might stay in their jobs because of it, but companies that see health care as only one step—and then add incentives such as a clean and healthy environment, respect for each employee, and recognition for a job well done—will not only retain these people, they'll enjoy increased productivity and loyalty.

Give Meaningful Incentives

Employees respond favorably to incentives, whether tangible or intangible. The promise of a bonus at the end of a productive year is a powerful motivator. So are awards for exceeding goals. A pat on the back will not do much for a grossly undercompensated employee, but a judicious blend of tangible incentives and psychological reward can work wonders.

One of the most popular forms of reward for good work has always been travel. This is in large measure because it rewards the employee's family as well. (Keeping employees' families happy and motivated is a vastly underrated retention tool.) If an employee's family is content with what he or she does, the employee is more likely to be content as well. Because travel is a strong incentive, I was particularly interested in a 1992 survey conducted by the Society of Incentive Travel Executives (SITE) Foundation, and reported in leading travel industry publications.

Eighty-nine percent of American workers responding to the survey felt their companies would be better off if employees were given meaningful incentives, but only 40 percent believed that the average American company currently offers such incentives. Further, 59 percent said the average company does not listen to their ideas.

What did they consider "meaningful incentives?" Cash ranked at the top of the list. Ninety-five percent cited a cash bonus as having the greatest motivational impact. Other less expensive and tangible rewards also ranked high. The survey revealed that

- 87 percent viewed special training as a positive incentive. (Which was heartening if you're in the least concerned about the skills shortage anticipated for the years ahead.)
- 85 percent considered stock options important.
- 77 percent of the respondents found a trip to a desirable destination with a spouse or guest to be appealing.
- 76 percent valued recognition at a company meeting.
- 63 percent ranked merchandise and a "pat on the back" as equally desirable.

An interesting parallel finding had to do with geography. Twenty percent more workers in the western United States valued praise as an important motivation than did employees in the Northeast.

HOW TO AVOID LOSING GOOD EMPLOYEES

When viewed from the perspective of management, those factors that influence employee motivation and performance naturally differ in relative weight and position. They aren't all *that* different, however.

Robert Half International did a survey in 1990 of executives in which they were asked whether they regretted losing an employee who'd been recruited by another company. Seventy percent replied affirmatively. Building on this, we asked executives to list what policies and procedures their companies had implemented to head off the recruitment of their good employees. Here is a summary of their responses:

33%	Competitive benefits
25%	Open communications
17%	Good work environment
8%	Incentive programs
8%	Periodic reviews/counseling
8%	Promotions/better job in another division

6%	Stock options
6%	Deferred compensation
6%	Management-by-objective programs
3%	Savings and matching programs
3%	Profit sharing

The differences that do exist between what employees want as incentives and what management is willing and able to give can be narrowed through listening on both sides. One thing is certain. If good employees are to be retained, it takes a commitment by management to keep them. The specifics might differ from company to company, but the effort must be made.

Commitment. A word that cuts two ways. What of employee commitment? How does a company foster it? After all, employee commitment and turnover are interlaced, and a lack of loyalty from employees is a strong prediction of turnover.

It's generally acknowledged that 70 percent of workers leave their jobs within the first three years of employment. Most quit after only a year. Based on these findings, not only do the first few weeks count in nurturing employee commitment, but also does the first day. My thoughts on structuring early days on the job are presented in the next chapter.

Some managers are "born motivators." They inspire loyalty and productivity by virtue of their dynamic leadership qualities. Others inspire quietly and generate employee loyalty and enhanced performance by example. All managers can learn to be more effective in bringing out the best in people. When they do, the revolving door slows down, and in many cases even ceases to turn for prolonged periods.

18

ORIENTATION AND TRAINING

Implementing Cross-Discipline Training

"Well done is rare."

How many new employees spend their first few days on the job shunted to an empty room where they're given employee handbooks and policy manuals to read? Everyone around them is working hard, but no one seems to have the time to *personally* ease them into the flow of the department and company.

New employees' first days should be planned. Written materials can always be taken home and read. It is more important to have new hires interact. Designate mentors (better yet, ask for volunteers) and free these people from routine tasks so that they can spend time with the newcomers, introducing them around and answering questions, not only about the company but also about seemingly mundane things that are nonetheless important—the best sandwich shop, the closest bank where company employees are welcome, where to order supplies, and how to structure expense reports.

Choose a few people to take new employees to lunch at company expense. It's also good to involve newcomers in their duties immediately; even small tasks give a sense of contributing. Above all, don't allow new employees to go home at the end of that first day feeling bored, confused, and unwelcomed. Getting off on the right foot pays dividends each day in the future.

ENCOURAGE CROSS-DISCIPLINE TRAINING

In the "good old days" when corporations were fully staffed and jobs were performed by functional definition, each person had a task and did it. The accounting staff accounted; the marketing staff marketed.

With downsizing, management finds itself having to meet increasingly difficult objectives with fewer workers. It's no longer sufficient for employees to function only in one narrowly defined area of responsibility. They must, in addition, understand the relationship of their function to all others in the company. The larger corporate goal has taken on greater significance.

Because of this, cross-discipline training has become an important and integral part of the current management approach at many companies. (An in-depth look at cross-discipline training is detailed by Robert Half International's chairman and CEO, Max Messmer, in the May, 1992, issue of *Management Review*.) Cross-discipline training makes good business sense for a number of reasons, two of which are increased productivity through improved communication and more strategic hiring decisions.

Increased Productivity

We've all experienced situations in which managers don't communicate with staff, and departments fail to do the same with other departments. Confusion, duplicated effort, and loss of morale are the inevitable result.

Training employees in multiple disciplines helps communications lines stay open. The result is reduced rivalry and increased cooperation. At the same time, the need for employee supervision decreases as workers develop a broader perspective on the entire company as well as their individual contribution to it. They begin to seek solutions to problems on their own, rather than depend solely on managerial intervention.

Better Hiring Decisions

Cross-discipline training also encourages more strategic and efficient hiring practices. Managers who spend time in each other's departments gain a better overall picture of companywide hiring needs and are less likely to fall prey to duplicated hiring and overstaffing. The resultant savings in payroll dollars can be put to better, more focused use, including the judicious utilization of part-time and temporary help. Should future downsizing be necessary, the more reasoned staffing approach accomplished through cross-discipline training results in a workforce of the proper strength. In addition, employees are prepared to shift gears and to expand their areas of responsibility. Fewer hands perhaps, but better ones.

GETTING MANAGEMENT COMMITMENT TO CROSS-DISCIPLINE TRAINING

Support for cross-discipline training must originate at the top. It won't work without management's genuine commitment, which isn't always easy to secure.

Some managers are naturally uncomfortable having to expose the inner recesses of their functional areas. Others resist having their staffs spend time elsewhere, claiming their departments are too busy to spare them; nor may they feel they have the extra time to train others who do not report directly to them.

That's why the upper reaches of management must be "sold" on the concept of cross-discipline training, especially in large corporations where fiefdoms are commonplace. The advantages to department managers should be emphasized. It's to their benefit to allow outsiders in and to send their staff to other departments for training. Managers gain new prestige by showcasing their department's capabilities to others, and having their own people more educated about how other departments function enhances their future contributions to the organization's overall health. If a company is only as good as its people, then it stands that people with a broad knowledge of the way a company functions will bring to it more enlightened leadership. In the process, managers expand their own careers. As added inducement for cooperation, managers who participate must be assured that they will not be penalized for any temporary lowering of department performance or production quotas.

Cross-discipline training costs time and money. For it to be effective over time, the financial resources needed to sustain it should be written directly into a company's overall budget. To guarantee this, departmental budgets should include a line item labeled "training," against which hours and equipment can be budgeted.

A particularly satisfying story of success brought about by cross-discipline training involved a timber company that had hired a number of financial and accounting personnel through Robert Half International. The manager of general accounting didn't end up in his position solely because his accounting credentials were strong. He took a different route.

He was hired directly out of college as a management trainee in Corporate Planning where he gained a broad overview of company operations. In the process, he developed valuable contacts with managers in numerous departments.

Two years later he was transferred to the marketing department where he had the opportunity to develop a new business line, which he took from zero revenues to $15 million in three years. By the time he applied his accounting education to heading the accounting division, he'd touched base with virtually every aspect of the company. His vision reached beyond purely working with numbers. He was equipped to lend valuable insight to a wide range of business decisions. For example, when facing the decision whether to close an unprofitable warehouse, the numbers said one thing. In addition to this he took into consideration that the warehouse provided a foothold in a competitive market (his marketing exposure), and that the long-range goals of the company were served by keeping it open (his planning experience). His value to the company had grown dramatically.

COMMUNICATE THE ADVANTAGES OF CROSS-DISCIPLINE TRAINING

Central to cross-discipline training is communication. If real information isn't exchanged, little is accomplished. Cross-training will not be successful if it is based on faulty and incomplete data or an unrealistic presentation of the way a department functions. It again comes back to instilling in every manager the sense that the objective of cross-training is not to identify weakness in the organization. To the contrary, the goal is to build strength on a systemwide basis. If someone from another division sees how things can be done more efficiently—based on his or her own area of expertise and need—everyone benefits. It might be hard for a manager to accept this, but if top management is committed to the concept, and has satisfactorily communicated its commitment, such personal concerns quickly abate and a closer team effort emerges.

Once on-board, managers should communicate the advantages of cross-discipline training to all employees:

- In the current uncertain economy, *security is greater* for a company whose employees have a "global" perspective. It stands to reason that the more adaptable a firm's employees, the more competitive the company. By extension, employees' career and professional potentials are broadened.

- Versatile employees can better engineer their own *career paths within the company*. Their growth is no longer restricted by the narrow functional arena in which they had operated. They know more people, and more things.

- When a company can't offer a promotion as a reward for a job well done, it can offer *greater exposure and increased responsibility* as an incentive. Salary should be adjusted to compensate for this new level of achievement. If there are a limited number of management positions to go around, employees can still be recognized for good performance.

- When a job is repetitive or detailed, rotation to other functional areas helps *eliminate stagnation and boredom*.

- By helping train co-workers, employees *clarify their own responsibilities*.

Bottom-Line Benefits

Although cross-discipline training is designed primarily to create a breed of employee with greater skills and knowledge, it can also have direct and swift impact on a company's bottomline.

A major consumer products company vigorously encouraged its marketing department to come up with a succession of new products. The department generated many creative ideas, many of which were then put through the expensive development phase to bring the products to market. Some of the ideas were successful; many weren't.

The company had been formulating plans for a long time to introduce cross-discipline training to selected employees. The first group that was exposed to it—members of the accounting and finance divisions—participated with the marketing department as it sought to create new product lines.

The co-mingling of these two disparate disciplines quickly showed results. Encouraged to provide input from the first day, the accountants offered valuable cost analysis to the new ideas, which ultimately cut down on the number of products subjected to expensive development. These sound accounting principles became ingrained in the marketing department's future thinking. At the same time, the accountants gained a greater appreciation for what the company hoped to accomplish by introducing new and improved products. Everyone benefitted, especially the company.

HIRE CANDIDATES RECEPTIVE TO CROSS-DISCIPLINE TRAINING

A commitment to cross-discipline training ideally should trickle down to the hiring process, with job candidates examined as much for their ability to grasp the proverbial big picture as for their technical competence. For a company committed to cross-discipline training, the strongest candidates will be multifaceted and amenable to change. It will seek to hire people whose natural curiosity and desire to grow is readily apparent.

There will always be a need, of course, for individuals who do not respond to such opportunities and who prefer to perform the single tasks for which they've been trained and hired. Any company with a preponderance of such people will find attempts at cross-discipline training difficult. The right employee mix, which includes enough people responsive to new vistas and learning opportunities, is what every company should try to achieve when hiring new employees, especially if cross-discipline training is in its future.

Accomplishing more with less has become the byword of business in the '90s. The recession at the onset of the decade created a new set of parameters; flexibility is paramount to success. Clinging to a rigid status quo is a formula for failure. Cross-discipline training provides a workable strategic solution.

19

THE SUGGESTION BOX IS NOT ENOUGH

Encouraging Employees' Ideas and Risk Taking

"Good ideas are not a monopoly of management."

To retain the best employees, a company must give them at least some role in decision making. By doing this, enlightened managers achieve a remarkably simple goal—they grant their employees the privilege of doing what they were hired to do in the first place.

An increasing number of companies have done more than talk about this. They've turned what originally was an interesting idea—listening to employee ideas and giving them the authority to implement the best of them—into an integral part of the workplace.

A national survey of 1000 employees, conducted by an independent research firm for Robert Half International in 1990, indicated that they believe managers are practicing what they preach when it comes to giving employees more input: 64 percent of employees claimed to have been given more authority to make decisions than they had been five years prior to the survey.

Geographically, employees in the Northeast, where many of America's oldest companies are headquartered, reported a greater change in management than did their counterparts elsewhere. The West, usually considered to be in the forefront of new workplace concepts, scored lowest of the four geographical regions.

The results of this survey are encouraging for those who advocate this approach, as I certainly do. However, a significant segment of American business must catch up if the concept is to be turned into workplace reality. There still remains 30 percent of employees who believe they've been given *less* authority than they had five years ago.

ENCOURAGE EMPLOYEES' SUGGESTIONS

Previously, the suggestion box represented the extent of employee input into operations and policies. In some cases it was exactly that, a forum through which employees could advance their ideas. The problem was, and still is with many companies, that it was a symbol rather than *an active participatory program*. Suggestions were given a cursory glance and then discarded.

For any philosophy of employee input to work, management must be committed to seriously considering all ideas. Suggestions needn't be accepted, but if employees learn that their suggestions aren't even considered, better ones will not be forthcoming. Nothing lowers employee morale faster than when management makes a *show* of listening to employees, but does nothing to actually implement their good ideas. Better to have no suggestion box at all than to use it as a bogus motivational tool.

I Power, published by Barricade Books, Inc. (1992), is a powerful book written by Martin Edelston, publisher of such popular informational newsletters as *Bottom Line/Personal* and *Boardroom Reports*. In *I Power* he outlines a suggestion system that has proved effective and extremely useful in his publishing company. By encouraging thousands of suggestions from his staff, the company has tripled its sales without increasing the number of employees, has practically eliminated turnover, has generated impressive profits, and boasts an inventory of excellent projects to be introduced over time.

The basic idea came from Peter Drucker, a foremost expert in management, who recommended, "Have everyone who comes to a meeting be prepared to give two ideas for making his/her own department's work more productive—ideas that will enhance the company as a whole."

For the system to work optimally, management is required to respond to *every* idea, good or bad. The system gets rolling with each employee offering two suggestions. They're read and evaluated weekly, and each worthwhile suggestion earns cash for the employee who came up with it—a dollar, five dollars, as much as 50 dollars. The money is not the motivational force, however. It's the excitement and spirit the system generates that makes it work. Accepted ideas can be as big as a concept for a new publication or as small as suggesting the need for larger wastebaskets.

Since the *I Power* system was initiated at Edelston's company four years ago, absenteeism and lateness have dropped significantly. It's a happy, spirited, productive place to work, and there continues to be no shortage of ideas. Each employee averages 200 of them in a year's time.

RESPOND TO EMPLOYEES' IDEAS FOR IMPROVEMENT

There invariably is a gap between how employees perceive management and how management perceives itself. This is especially true where ideas and suggestions from employees are concerned.

Managers of 200 of the nation's largest companies were asked in 1990 if they believed they currently gave employees more authority to make decisions and to take action than they did five years ago. A resounding 88 percent claimed they did. (As mentioned, 64 percent of employees in our survey felt that way.)

The difference between employee and management responses could be due to a variety of factors. The acceptance of input might have increased for some employees, but not enough to cause them to answer in the affirmative. In such cases, it's incumbent on management to do a better job of communicating the changes it has instituted.

On the other hand, it could be that management believes it has responded fairly to employee ideas, but hasn't in any tangible manner. This often occurs when individual managers attempt to listen to employee ideas in a company atmosphere of, for the most part, rigid hierarchical authority.

Being open to employee ideas within a department can help to an extent, but the overall impact is muffled unless the concept and its implementation, fueled by upper management's firm commitment, is endorsed companywide. Like cross-discipline training, management buy-in is essential.

ENCOURAGE EMPLOYEES TO TAKE RISKS

The philosophy that encourages employee input inherently demands a certain level of prudent risk taking on everyone's part, coupled with the assurance that no one will be penalized for failure. The "permission" to take prudent risks must emanate from the top. Otherwise, visionary middle managers who wish to encourage their employees to take risks will be reluctant to do so. If, on the other hand, those same middle managers are encouraged by their superiors to reach for success through prudent risk taking, they'll be significantly more comfortable urging their people to do the same.

More than the concept must be "sold" to upper management, however. As with any effective presentation, the benefits need to be explained in tangible, not vague, terms.

- What projected increase in the bottom-line might reasonably be expected?
- Will the projected increase in employee morale and productivity justify the investment required to implement a program of this scope?
- Will costly turnover be reduced?

Equally as important as covering projected benefits is the analysis of realistic parameters for risk taking. The determination of how much risk and failure will be tolerated must be established and codified to the extent that it is clear and understandable to management and to those employees who are directly involved.

If properly presented, a program such as this might be approved on a trial basis. That's good enough, provided that the period of time allowed is sufficient for the program to show results, and that management support is greater than half-hearted.

Once the concept has been bought, it's time for middle managers to call their people together to lay out the agreed-upon guidelines. Specificity is important. How far will they be allowed to reach? What levels of risk are acceptable?

Early in any formal program, employees should be encouraged to discuss with their managers those "risky" ventures they contemplate undertaking. This is not intended to stifle initiative. Rather, early involvement between employee and manager is designed to enhance the potential for success of ideas that have an element of prudent risk. Managers, using their experience, might make suggestions that strengthen the employee's idea, rather than stand in its way.

This early interaction also helps to clarify the structure of the program and its limits. Once those factors are more fully understood and the program has been in operation for a period of time, less managerial interjection is usually necessary. Employees are able to recognize that they have been given *real* power to help shape not only the company's future, but also their own.

FOSTER TRUST BETWEEN MANAGERS AND EMPLOYEES

The biggest potential problem is obvious. If managers give the green light for employees to take prudent risks, and then become critical if failures result from those decisions, the worth of the program is not only diminished, a destructive field of distrust is created. Better never to have initiated a plan than to put it into effect, and then back off on promises.

Companies that enthusiastically support employee risk taking take the concept of encouraging prudent risk a step further. They've established various forms of rewarding "smart risks," even if those risks do not result in success. What this says to employees is that the company not only believes in its employees ideas, but also is sincere when it says that prudent risk is encouraged. Those who seize the opportunity but fail need not fear repercussions. In fact, they might even receive a bonus for their efforts.

It's axiomatic that the more employees feel a true part of a company, the harder they'll work to achieve its goals. They have to know what those goals are, however. An open and ongoing communication must exist at all levels and flow both up and down the chain of command.

Trust should flow both ways, too. Without it, even the best conceived plans of employee motivation and retention fail to achieve their true potentials.

Listening to employees and allowing (even encouraging) them to take risks isn't just a nice idea, it's already in practice in thousands of businesses across America. Those companies that have already embraced it are enjoying the fruits of higher morale, increased productivity from leaner staffs, a marked decrease in employee turnover, and, ultimately, a stronger bottomline. When employees are given enough latitude to achieve their full potential, a company's full potential is likely to be realized as well.

20

ATTITUDE PROBLEMS: THEM AND US

Listening to Employees

"We never did it that way before."

Every book that addresses the subject of employee motivation naturally touches on employee attitudes, but what about *employer* attitudes? Little is written about that subject, primarily because of the "them and us" perception that characterizes too many companies.

I'd be the last to deny the need for a clearly defined management structure. We all need to know what is expected of us in our jobs, the level at which we must perform in order to keep those jobs, and the person or people to whom we report.

Over the years, however, that concept of hierarchy has led many otherwise good managers to adopt an authoritarian stance. "Just do it," they respond when asked for reasons. When approached with ideas that might better accomplish a task, they often automatically ignore them because they didn't come from them. Their *attitude* is defined by their position in the hierarchy, which has historically dictated that attitude problems must, of necessity, rest with those reporting to them. It is this brand of manager who invariably suffers the greatest employee morale problems; it is their revolving doors that turn faster.

WHAT MOTIVATES EMPLOYEES HAS CHANGED

I acknowledge the need for accountability to a higher power. Everyone has a boss. A company's CEO must report to a board of directors. Even a board of directors has a boss—the consumer of the company's products and services.

Times have irrefutably changed, however, and "business as usual" is no longer a viable way to proceed. Most changes are due to outside forces that shape American business. In response, attempts are made to initiate new and innovative policies to accomplish goals in this altered climate. Unless the general attitude of a company's management changes for the better toward employee motivation and retention, these attempts at enlightened leadership stand little chance of succeeding. What prevails in too many cases is the notion that if it was good enough before, it's good enough now. The simple truth is that some of the "good old ways" weren't very good at all.

Today's workers are different than their parents. Their needs and expectations, shaped by changes in the environment in which they grew up, are certainly not the same as those of previous generations. Of course, some older workers are dismayed by what they perceive as a diminished work ethic, but that assessment is wrong for the most part.

What *has* changed are the factors that motivate today's workers. The gold watch and the pension are not as compelling as they once were (although a decent retirement and recognition for a job well done are never out of style). A Thanksgiving turkey and family picnic are pleasant pluses, but do not foster employee loyalty and commitment as they once did. The following sections address the needs and expectations that motivate employees of the 1990s.

INVOLVE EMPLOYEES IN KEY DECISIONS THAT AFFECT THEIR WORK

Today's workers possess a heightened sense of individuality. Many may be called on to perform duties by rote, but at the same time they have ideas about how to make their jobs and the company better. They view their employment as more of a partnership than did previous generations, which were more comfortable with the traditional employer-employee relationship. Today's workers still respect the need for management structure and chain of command, but they don't consider it as an obstacle to their perceived partnership.

Employees in these times "want in." They wish to feel a part of a company's success and to have their contributions recognized. They seek the opportunity to advance ideas, good and bad, and be told why their ideas have been adopted or shelved. They expect answers and deserve them. Any company concerned about retaining and motivating its good people should be willing, indeed anxious, to meet this expectation, not because of some vague altruistic philosophy but because *it's good business*.

Why are so many employees left out of the loop when it comes to decisions that directly affect their everyday working lives?

Suppose new equipment is purchased for a factory, or an office is redesigned. However, those who work in them every day are not consulted for their knowledge of what must be accomplished. Inviting the rank-and-file to contribute to such projects does not mandate accepting their suggestions, but their ideas might have made the new office or factory more efficient and palatable. If that were the case, not only would the company function more smoothly and productively, those same employees would feel they are a more integral part of its operations and goals.

For example, the owner of a restaurant I occasionally visit decided to redesign its bar area. The bartender had worked there for 20 years, yet, when the designs were developed, he was never consulted. As a result, his job was made more difficult because things were no longer located where they functionally should have been. Worse, he was demoralized. By not recognizing this veteran bartender's years of professional experience, the owner conveyed the impression—right or wrong—that he didn't hold his good employee in especially high regard. The bartender's ideas did not have to be accepted, but he should have been asked.

Here's another example. Years ago I made a routine visit to the Los Angeles office of Robert Half International. Its manager, who'd been with us for many years, brought up a problem he was having with his second in command, an extremely capable woman. It certainly wasn't an earth-shattering problem: He believed that her desk was situated in a location that made it difficult for her to supervise some key people who reported to her. "If I tell her to move it," he told me, "she'll get angry."

I suggested we go to dinner and return to the office later. "No one will be there," I said. "We can move her desk to see if it will work the way you think it will."

After dinner, we returned and moved the desk to the new location. The manager was right. It was a better spot for her desk, but before we left the office, we moved everything back to the way it had been earlier in the day.

I spoke with the woman the next morning about a number of routine administrative matters. Then I asked her to suggest things that would make her work easier and more efficient. As if it were an afterthought, I said, "Can you think of a better spot for your desk?"

Her response: "I've been thinking it might be better over there." She pointed to the spot her manager and I had moved it to the night before. We relocated it before she changed her mind.

Good workers don't especially like to be told to do something different. They naturally resist change, but if you can get them to come up with the idea as though it were their own, two people are made happy—you and the employee.

One final example: a friend of mine owns a one-man import-export company. He hired a part-time employee a number of years ago and soon was aware that she was often sullen and without energy. He finally realized that he'd been telling her how to do everything. That was his nature. He eventually established a more interactive relationship. She was informed of what had to be accomplished and was encouraged to accomplish it, using her own approach. The change in her attitude was dramatic. She brimmed with verve and purpose, and a lot more got done.

CRITICIZE CAREFULLY AND CONSTRUCTIVELY

The way in which we criticize employees is an excellent barometer of how things have changed (or should have changed) in today's business environment. The "business as usual" approach assumes the right to criticize those reporting to superiors. That's the way it's always been. However, if we buy into the concept of employee input and risk-taking—and every indication points to it as setting the tone for the future—the ability to "criticize" must flow in two directions, up *and* down.

Unfortunately, the connotation of terms such as *criticize* and *evaluate* gets in the way. They ring negative because they traditionally were used in a negative fashion. Employee evaluations were considered to be the opportunity for management to point out employee inadequacies. It was a one-way street. No wonder employees viewed the yearly "report card" with trepidation and disdain.

Today, the management of companies that have embraced a more forward-looking philosophy of employee evaluations see it as a time to exchange information, to analyze and discuss collectively how the employee can play a greater role in the company's future, and to correct deficiencies that might stand in the way of achieving that. (Chapter 21 presents a blueprint for conducting effective employee evaluations.)

Bill Marriott of the Marriott Hotel chain has set a new standard where evaluations are concerned. Although the company conducts regular reviews of all employees' performance, it also dispatches Marriott's top executives to a one-day retreat where their only task is to critique Bill Marriott. I understand that he takes their comments very much to heart and acts on many of them.

Few of us enjoy criticizing others, but it comes with the territory of being a manager. It simply has to be done. Criticism isn't all bad. Ultimately it's the manner in which it's handled that can be detrimental to working relationships.

Offer constructive criticism. For example, if a report submitted by an employee is inadequate, try saying, "You're on the right track, but you need to include more information and to work on the style of presentation." That will generate a more positive response than, "Do the report over again and make sure it's complete this time." Sometimes, as in this case, it's just a matter of qualifying what's said. To take further demoralizing aspects out of criticism, focus the discussion on the task, not the person.

Ask yourself the following questions to see what kind of a critic you are:

1. Do you make sure you've got all the facts before confronting an employee?
2. Do you exert your best effort to be constructive?
3. Do you make it a point to say something complimentary before getting to the criticism?
4. Do you try, when appropriate, to assume part of the responsibility for mistakes?
5. Do you stick to the issues and eliminate personalities?
6. Do you remain objective and listen to the other side of the story?
7. Are you sarcastic when criticizing?
8. Do you make it a point to criticize employee when others are around?

9. Do you lose your temper easily?

10. Do you always contradict the employee?

If you answered "yes" to questions 1 through 6, your approach to criticism is constructive and should be effective. Questions 7 through 10 indicate a negative approach to criticism—an approach that should be avoided. Above all, keep in mind that the purpose of criticism is to promote goodwill, prevent recurrence, teach better skills, and improve efficiency.

STAND UP FOR YOUR EMPLOYEES' IDEAS

Anyone who's been in the business world for any amount of time has run into two types of managers: those who stand squarely behind their employees and those who back them only when they're right and abandon them when they're wrong.

Willis Player, who was vice president of public relations for Pan American World Airlines during its high-flying days, once summed up his philosophy to a friend of mine who had worked directly for him. Player's philosophy was that his primary responsibility was to hire the right people and make sure upper management knew how good they were. He constantly crowed about their achievements. When someone failed, he stood firmly behind that individual's *right to fail*. His message to his superiors was that he'd hired the best, and the airline was fortunate to have such people working for it.

How many good ideas are never advanced to a level of management at which they can be implemented because of fear that someone further up the chain of command won't like them? If a company's prevailing atmosphere is one of fear of failure rather than the encouragement of prudent risk taking, good ideas are routinely scrapped at lower levels. Safer to say "no" than to run the risk of having a superior say it.

DON'T AUTOMATICALLY SAY "NO" TO AN EMPLOYEE'S IDEA

The word *No* can be a powerful deterrent to business success. Companies that equate safety with negativism create what's come to be known as a "No"-Zone layer, a cloud of negativity under which all employees must function. (Max Messmer, chairman and CEO of Robert Half International, spelled out how a "No"-Zone layer develops in companies in his excellent article in the November, 1989, issue of *Accounting Today*.)

What basically happens in this atmosphere is that initiative wanes, risk is avoided at all costs, and ideas drown. Worse, a "No"-Zone layer thickens over time, fed by the repeated "no" employees hear whenever they present an idea that threatens the status quo.

A "No"-Zone layer is created and fed with management responses such as

"You're right. That would save time for everyone, but the change would require too much disruption."

"I like the idea but Ben in marketing will never buy it. Let's not even bring it up."

"Great idea. Let's think about setting up a task force to explore it."

"That would definitely be helpful, but it'll cost money. Let's wait and see if we come in under budget somewhere else."

Try to avoid such responses. Admittedly, most ideas are *not* worth pursuing to the stage of implementation: they prove to be impractical or run counter to long-range goals. However, that can never be determined unless there is an open field for them to be expressed and fairly evaluated by all the right people at the right levels.

It isn't only the ideas that merit consideration in the hope that some will prove to be profitable. It's the people behind those ideas who deserve, indeed need, to know that their thinking counts. When they do, spirits soar, productivity rises, and the revolving door turns less frequently.

"No"-Zone layers are insidious in that they just seem to appear before anyone notices. Then, inertia fuels them until they become an ingrained and integral part of a company's operational atmosphere. Obviously, the time to begin dismantling the "No"-Zone layer is before it gets started.

Undoubtedly, there will be managers in the most enlightened and forward-looking companies who, by virtue of previous experience and ingrained philosophies, create their own private "No"-Zone layers. When a company as an entity stands firm against such pockets of negativity, however, it's more difficult for them to be sustained.

Although upper reaches of management must set the tone that discourages "No"-Zone layers, it's up to managers at every level to implement that philosophy. The entrepreneurial spirit that encourages individual problem solving and risk taking stems from people, not from organization charts.

Here are a few of the principles and approaches that will help managers encourage employees and, by extension, discourage "No"-Zone layers.

- Ask managers to regularly second-guess themselves. Have ideas generated by employees been shrugged off or shelved because they were too much trouble to pursue? When turning down ideas, have the reasons for doing so been properly explained to the contributing employees? Have those same people been encouraged to submit other ideas, and are they confident they'll be given a reasonable hearing?

- Are ideas that look good on the surface given a full airing and hashed out in an open and free atmosphere of give-and-take? The most visionary and creative ideas often sound ridiculous when first uttered. It's only through discussion that their true merit can be determined and fine-turned. This takes a willingness by managers to be open-minded, even to the extent of acknowledging that their immediate negative responses might have been wrong. Once employees realize that their superiors are open to exploring new ideas and are willing to expose their own thinking, the creative process is enhanced.

- Are managers committed to carrying good ideas to a higher level, one at which implementation is more likely? If so, will the appropriate credit be given to the employee who originated the idea? I have always believed that one of the management traits employees view most favorably is a boss who'll go to bat for them and who'll take the necessary steps to make things happen.

- Are all employees aware of the company's commitment to encouraging new and innovative ideas? This responsibility rests with individual managers. Having conceptually "banned" the "No"-Zone layer from a company is only the first step, albeit a critically important one. Unless there is an active field at all levels in which ideas are openly sought, good ideas will be slow in coming. The most effective managers I know have initiated tangible and visible programs to elicit ideas from employees. They schedule regular sessions at which the "podium" is open to all. People are *expected* to come to these sessions with ideas.

Employees soon get this message: The company values you and your ideas and expects you to contribute them.

- Do managers have enough of the evangelist in them to fire up their employees?

- Does the company believe that strategy is the art of experimentation and encourage its employees to take prudent risks to achieve bigger and better results? Has each manager truly bought into this concept, and are employees comfortable knowing that if they risk and fail, they won't be punished? Any manager uncomfortable with taking risk might consider that turtles only make progress when they stick their necks out.

- Is the commitment to abolishing the "No"-zone layer genuine or is it like those suggestion boxes into which go ideas that will never be considered?

- Is there a tendency to seek safety in numbers? Are ideas routinely saved up to be presented to a task force? Nothing discourages ideas faster than knowing they'll be picked apart by many people. Unless someone champions ideas at such meetings, they're doomed to fail. Remember: A meeting is no substitute for progress. In most cases, task forces serve only to delay action.

- Is every manager willing to admit mistakes? In 1992 Robert Half International commissioned a survey of executives at 200 large American companies. They indicated that lower-level staff employees are more willing to admit mistakes than are their bosses. This inevitably results in an unmotivated and risk-shy workforce. Admitting mistakes is the best way to avoid repeating them. Henry Ford forgot to put a reverse gear in his first automobile. Edison invested over $2 million in an invention that didn't work. Neither of these great men made those same mistakes again. We can view mistakes as Robert W. Johnson, founder of Johnson & Johnson, did. "If I wasn't making mistakes," he said, "I wasn't making decisions."

- Is the humor quotient of a department sufficiently high to help boost morale when risk results in failure? No one would suggest that managers be responsible for comic relief, but those who are self-effacing enough to laugh at their own mistakes and foibles set a tone that eases tension and contributes to departmental harmony.

TREAT EMPLOYEES WITH KINDNESS

Let's not forget human kindness. Kindness will never substitute for a woefully inadequate salary and benefits structure, yet some of the most loyal employees I've known worked in situations in which the pay and benefits were not up to par. They arrived early and stayed late, took on projects that were beyond their responsibility and, in general, were exemplary employees. The reasons? Their bosses were kind people who gave them a deserved day off, showed up at family funerals, visited the hospital, and remembered to buy birthday, anniversary, and other gifts that had personal meaning for the employees. These bosses also were quick to say "thank you" for a job well done.

On the other hand, if kindness reeks of manipulation, it will have the opposite effect. I once knew an executive who programmed his calendar to remind himself to ask his employees every three months about their families. This is akin to computers sending birthday cards to clients for business reasons.

Long before there were comprehensive benefit packages, I knew a partner in an accounting firm who, when a loyal employee had sickness in the family, directed that the firm pay all medical expenses and that the employee be given as many days off as needed to attend to the situation. Neither he nor the company broadcast this, but the word got around. So did the fact that the executive in the previous example, the man with notations on his calendar to "demonstrate kindness and concern," obviously didn't mean it when he asked about the spouse and kids.

PRAISE EMPLOYEES

Why is it that so many managers find it difficult to praise their employees? The answer may be attributed to some vague and questionable school of management that teaches that too much praise creates complacency—the school of "keep them on edge."

A better school teaches that it's virtually impossible to over-praise. Most employees respond to praise by working harder. Similarly, those who work hard but feel unappreciated are likely to cut back on their efforts.

Jealousy, envy, disappointment, anger, joy, fear, ambition, pettiness, love, hate, inadequacy—the gamut of human emotions is as active in the workplace as in the home and community. What should matter to a company is that these human feelings be channeled in a positive direction, one in which the individual and company find room and reason to grow.

Employees who are empowered to create and contribute have less reason to vent their frustration. Those who are encouraged to take prudent risks without fear of undue reprisal seek new heights, not only for themselves but for their companies.

Above all else, the problems inherent in these things that make us human are not restricted to *employees*. They are shared by everyone in the company, CEO and mailroom clerk alike. When the human community that *is* a company sees itself as linked to a common goal and purpose and acts accordingly, growth follows. What more can any company ask?

21

THAT DREADED TIME OF THE YEAR

Evaluating Employee Performance

"Everyone wants an Oscar."

A major problem with employee reviews is that too many professionals and clerical employees don't understand how their work is evaluated or even what periodic appraisals are meant to accomplish. When employees are unsure of the reason for performance reviews, management itself either lacks understanding of their purpose or has failed to communicate it to those being evaluated. In either case, companies fail to enjoy the primary benefit of a solid, carefully considered employee review system—strengthened employee performance.

USE PERFORMANCE REVIEWS TO MOTIVATE, NOT TO CRITICIZE

To be truly effective, periodic reviews must be perceived by employee and company alike as *positive* management tools. When this is achieved, the influence upon superior people to stay with the company is enhanced considerably.

Some managers approach review time (every six months in some companies) as an opportunity to criticize. Often the reviews are the only time an employee's shortcomings are addressed. Complaints about performance are compiled and presented as a litany of dissatisfaction. There are so many negative points to cover that there's scant time for praise and, more important, discussion of future goals and the employee's role in reaching them. It is no small wonder so many employees dread review time.

However, they're not the only ones who wince when the calendar indicates it's time for reviews. I've known managers who approach the task with all the enthusiasm of going to war. To be fair, many of them are required to conduct reviews under an entrenched system that renders the task more ominous and difficult than it needs to be. If there is also a lack of ongoing give-and-take between superior and subordinate, the problem is compounded.

It's my contention that scheduled reviews should be nothing more than a time to *formalize* what has been achieved over the course of six months. Employees should not be "judged" twice a year. That there is a need at all to formalize employee evaluations has been exacerbated by the litigious climate in which business has found itself. Formal reviews offer legal protection for employers should it become necessary to dismiss an employee. If the employee's lack of performance and, perhaps, attitudinal problems have been duly noted during reviews, a better case can be made for dismissal. An even better case can be built if an employee's inadequacies are discussed and noted on a more frequent basis than once or twice a year.

No one likes to be judged, especially when a job or promotion could be on the line, and few of us enjoy being in the position of having to evaluate another person's worth. At any rate, a formal system of review is a necessary ingredient of effective management. Without it, especially in larger companies, employee responsibilities are less clearly defined, and company objectives are similarly blurred.

A useful employee review should be multifold, affording both employer and employee a chance to see where things stand between them and to solidify their relationship. In addition, it can and should serve as a valuable motivational tool.

Another major reason so many managers enter into employee evaluations with a large bottle of antacid nearby concerns the paperwork involved. Here is where scrutiny and revision of forms can pay sizable dividends for everyone involved. Although no one would argue the necessity of a standardized form to inject uniformity into the process, is the information called for really necessary to accomplish the goal of motivating employees to reach their potential? In many cases, it isn't. Simplifying the paperwork not only relieves managers of an undue and unnecessary burden, it helps ensure a more accurate evaluation of employees. Less is more, as the saying goes.

A final word about employee review forms. Sometimes, managers rely too heavily on them, eschewing the need for more regular face-to-face contact. When this happens, the review process turns into assigning "grades." This is not only counterproductive, it's demeaning and confusing for the person being evaluated.

REVIEW PERFORMANCE GOALS

Unless managers clearly understand each employee's responsibilities, it's difficult to conduct an effective review. This may sound axiomatic but it's too often ignored. For a review to reflect accuracy, an individual's performance should be assessed only in regard to specified goals. Granted, there are numerous less tangible factors to be considered, but unless a manager has a full understanding of what an employee is supposed to do, how can it be decided whether the employee has done it? (The value of that carefully crafted and thought-out job description proves itself once again.)

The purpose of a review must be clear in the manager's mind and be made clear to employees, preferably ahead of time. This not only puts employees at ease, but also simplifies things for the manager. Like a good interview, an employee review should focus on a minimal number of objectives, the most important of which is to encourage each individual to perform to a higher standard.

While many managers structure in-person employee reviews based on aspects of the individual's appointed tasks and responsibilities, there is a growing number who prefer to view performance in terms of the past, the present, and the future. For them, discussing job performance is only worthwhile if strengths and weaknesses are keyed to the demands of the moment and, more important, what the future holds for the department and company.

To my knowledge, managers who espouse this approach generally apportion approximately 25 percent of the review to past performance, perhaps 15 percent to the present, and the greater percentage to future goals and expectations. These percentages will, of course, vary from manager to manager, but it is the *future* that should receive the most attention:

- What must each employee be prepared to do to attain the company's future goals?

- What deficiencies currently exist that might get in their way?
- What remedies are available to correct those deficiencies?

Employees whose performances are seriously under-par pose the biggest problem. If there has been regular dialogue throughout the year, the task is made easier at review time. No matter how difficult it is to confront an employee about serious inadequacies (especially a nice employee), it must be done in a forthright and clear manner. Two important things are at stake.

First, failing to bring up negative points that could impact on an employee's future employment does that person an injustice. Most people like to know where they stand, even if their standing at that moment isn't favorable.

The second consideration must be the manager's own career. An employee's failure to produce as part of a team places the manager in jeopardy, not only because work isn't completed satisfactorily, but also because the work of others on the team is invariably compromised.

A negative evaluation demands back-up and documentation. Chronic lateness or absenteeism cannot be discussed effectively as a vague concept. Provide dates and times. Discussing a succession of missed deadlines only has impact when specifics are laid on the table.

Subsequent regular meetings with an employee whose performance is sub-standard, but whose motivation and attitude are positive, may result in eventual improvement. A good worker, despite areas of weakness, is worth keeping, provided, of course, that the weaknesses can be corrected and the employee wishes to correct them. The manager in this situation must also make a commitment to help the individual grow. This takes patience, the amount of which can only be determined by demands on the department and its workers. When patience pays off in a better employee, the results are rewarding for all concerned.

WHAT TO DO WHEN PERSONAL PROBLEMS AFFECT PERFORMANCE

Not all employee problems stem from work. Perplexing personal challenges can arise and adversely impact job performance. A marriage may be in trouble. A parent could be facing major surgery or suffering from a terminal disease. A child is having trouble in school. An employee's debts have gotten out of hand. Perhaps alcohol or drug addiction could be the underlying problem. The right approach to take with good employees whose work has suffered because of personal problems has been the source of management debate for years. On the one hand, there is human compassion to be considered. On the other, there are businesses to be run.

The answer depends, of course, on myriad factors. For example, how long has the individual worked for the company, and during that time has the standard of performance been sufficiently high? It's often easier to help an employee get over a personal problem than to seek a replacement. When this approach works, the company retains a good employee, and a worthwhile human being is salvaged.

It isn't always easy to determine whether a personal problem is at the root of diminished performance. It takes keeping an ear to the grapevine (which managers should do anyway in order to stay informed). Although employee grapevines are rife with erroneous rumor, they are also the source of a surprising amount of good information. In addition, a good manager should be alert to changes in an employee's behavior pattern. A sudden spate of lateness or absenteeism by someone who has not demonstrated such behavior in the past could be a sign that something has changed in that person's life. (Various community and self-help groups are a good source of information on telltale signs of possible drug or alcohol abuse.)

Handling Substance Abuse Problems

Company policy toward helping employees with addictions will run the gamut from instant dismissal to company-sponsored support groups. In many cases, the human resources department will refer employees with such problems to outside agencies. In smaller firms, this offer is made by individual managers.

What's most important is that a company develop a sound policy that bridges the gap between undue harshness and excessive acceptance of untoward behavior and diminished performance.

Decades ago, the Union Carbide Corporation, in concert with physicians and Alcoholics Anonymous, developed an approach to alcoholic employees that embraced what became known as "tough love." An extensive training program was launched to enable managers to detect alcoholics within their employee ranks. The method of confrontation was codified and taught. The message was: "We value you and your contributions to the company, but your problem with alcohol has impacted on your work. We want you to seek help, and we stand ready to support you while you recover. If you choose not to seek help, we'll have no choice but to terminate you."

Union Carbide meant what it said in this visionary program. Employees were backed as long as they participated in structured recovery programs. Those who chose not to avail themselves of the company's generous offer were dismissed, which often was sobering enough to send them for help on their own.

REVIEWS CAN HELP RETAIN GOOD EMPLOYEES

With today's leaner workforce, companies might not have the luxury of "carrying" problem employees. Only a reasoned evaluation of an individual's worth to the company can determine whether an altruistic program for such people will, over time, benefit the company.

For less serious personal problems, managers are usually called on to be counselors, therapists, or clergy. Again, extending this extra effort can help a company retain otherwise productive and loyal employees.

One thing seems certain. For a manager to be truly effective, every effort must be made to separate strictly professional and job-related problems from those fueled by personal anxiety. Good people are hard to find. Once you have them, walking the proverbial extra mile can be smart business.

Union Carbide's program was predicated on the belief that to avoid confronting a problem employee head-on is to do that person and the company an injustice. What invariably happens when problems are ignored is a subtle mistreatment of the employee. The manager becomes distant, hands that individual unpleasant and increasingly meaningless assignments, and, in general, creates a tense and adversarial atmosphere, and is usually not even aware that he or she is doing this. The result? The employee becomes confused and even less productive because of the manager's passive-aggressive behavior. No one wins.

Because of the current changes in the way business must function, the manner in which business leaders deal with and motivate the workforce must also change. The employee review is one area in which great strides can be made. Using it to find fault accomplishes little, but utilizing to inspire workers to reach new heights in their careers almost always brings about a parallel improvement in company performance.

22

PROMOTIONS AND TITLES: WHO GETS WHAT?

Recognizing Good Performance

"Recognition is an honor money can't buy."

The need to promote employees in order to retain them often results from a policy that precludes promoting from within. It also happens within departments that do not have a fair and reasonable system for judging who is ready for promotion. Good people who have consistently proved themselves qualified become frustrated when openings occur but are filled with less qualified colleagues or by new hires from outside. These valuable employees will see "the writing on the wall," and many will seek opportunity elsewhere.

WHEN TO PROMOTE EMPLOYEES

The question of when to promote employees has always been problematic. Countless formulas have been devised, each reflecting diverse corporate philosophy. Basically, people are promoted for one (or all) of five reasons:

1. To fill or strengthen a position
2. To reward a good employee

3. To retain a good employee
4. To overcome salary caps
5. To honor seniority

Let's take them in order.

Promoting to Fill or Strengthen a Position

This should be the primary motivation for promoting someone. If the right person is primed for a move up, and that person's qualifications fit the job specs, the decision is relatively easy. It's the other four reasons that cause the most managerial anguish.

Promoting to Reward a Good Employee

It's been my experience that promoting an employee as a reward for good work seldom accomplishes much. The major problem in rewarding-through-promotion is that unless the employee has demonstrated the increased capacity to take on greater responsibility, a promotion can move that individual into the land of "The Peter Principle," coined a number of years ago by Laurence J. Peter. Mr. Peter's thesis was that we are too often promoted to our "level of incompetence." For example, an excellent classroom teacher is rewarded by being named principal, the administrative demands of which are beyond the scope of that person's abilities or interest. Consequently, a wonderful teacher is lost, and a mediocre principal is created.

A former corporate psychiatrist for Western Electric, Howard Hess, took exception with Laurence Peter's contention. Hess feels that people are promoted to their level of "pain," not incompetence. They reach a threshold of success that they are not emotionally equipped to handle.

Incompetence or pain aside, the salient point is that rewarding people by promoting them can result in placing the wrong person in the wrong job, a situation calculated to be detrimental to a department's functioning.

Promoting to Retain a Good Employee

Using promotions to retain good people and boost their morale can create similar problems unless the process is carefully considered and structured. Here, I am not talking about a reward for having performed a specific task well. There are short-term ways in which to say "thanks"—

a small bonus, theater or sporting event tickets, an extra day off, or a featured article in a company publication.

Using a promotion to retain a good employee should only be considered if the person has proven to be a loyal and productive employee, one management would hate to lose. The key is that the job to which the employee is elevated be compatible with his or her capabilities, or that the employee not actually assume new duties and responsibilities but be given a "promotion" in title only.

Promoting to Overcome Salary Caps

This reason is a natural outgrowth of current corporate lean-and-mean staffing considerations. The number of slots to which employees can be promoted, with accompanying raises, have become fewer as staffs are culled to reach leaner levels. Fewer jobs means fewer legitimate opportunities to advance within a company.

Salary caps can create a need to promote employees in order to retain them when meaningful salary increases can't be given. If raises aren't an option, there must be some sort of compensating recognition to motivate and retain deserving employees. Failing that, more employees will enter the revolving door.

Promoting an Employee to Honor Seniority

The fifth reason to promote generally proves to be self-defeating. Unless the person with seniority has the talent or desire for the more demanding job, the company is likely to condemn this otherwise good employee to a destiny of eventual failure. At the same time, others in the department ultimately become resentful and restless because they may perceive that mere stamina leads to promotion, not merit and hard work. They may begin looking for jobs elsewhere.

GIVING JOB TITLES TO RECOGNIZE EFFECTIVE PERFORMANCE

Titles can do wonders for employee morale. Not only do they provide a sense of function and stature within a company, their value extends well beyond the workplace. New acquaintances don't ask how much money a person makes (at least etiquette says they shouldn't), but job titles are readily exchanged in conversation. Families carry with them the pride of a member's title. Our titles at work become an integral part of who we are as we proceed through our lives.

British tabloids enjoy poking fun at royalty, but a 1990 Robert Half International survey confirms that attaining "corporate royalty" is viewed by a cross-section of employees as the second greatest indication of status at a company. (It should come as no surprise that compensation was chosen as the primary indicator. I wonder whether the majority of respondents to the survey focused on "status." Work titles are known to many others; salaries are known to a select few.)

Salary aside, the following percentages show how the respondents rated status:

Title	52 percent
Proximity to CEO	19 percent
Size of staff supervised	8 percent
Office size	6 percent
Office furnishings	2 percent
Some other indicator/Don't know	13 percent

In response to an additional question, 53 percent of the executives queried felt that inflated job titles had increased over the previous five years. Titles that fail to illuminate the actual responsibility inherent in them, or that are bestowed indiscriminately, do a disservice to those possessing legitimate, meaningful ones. Companies that are guilty of passing out an overabundance of inflated titles also suffer. Awarding credible titles is an acceptable motivational and retention tool when other means of recognition and compensation aren't available.

If a title is *created* in order to motivate a good person to stay, care should be taken not to reach beyond the mainstream of titles already within the company. Some companies are capable of coming up with bizarre employee titles. Consider these from a 1991 survey of 200 executives from 1000 of America's largest companies; they were asked to report on the most unusual job titles they'd come across:

- Graffiti Removal Trainee
- Grand Mogul
- Vice President and Ombudsman of Social Responsibility
- Semi-Senior Auditor

Employees don't want silly titles. Worthwhile job titles shouldn't need clarification; expounding, perhaps, but never clarification.

We've all heard jokes and complaints about companies handing out impressive titles without an accompanying increase in salary. Be that as it may, the fact is that titles *are* extremely important to most people. While they may joke about a new title sans higher salary, they instinctively recognize that loftier titles carry with them inherent rewards, including the possibility of tangible ones at a later date.

Savvy employees, when handed a new title without an accompanying salary increase, won't make jokes about it. They know that once they possess the title, an increase in salary might not be far behind. They also realize that each elevation in title makes it easier to go after the next higher rung on the ladder. When an assistant vice president is promoted to vice president, the opportunity probably would not have been available if the "assistant" title hadn't been offered and accepted earlier.

The importance of job titles is further underlined in a survey taken by *Personnel Journal*, reported in its March, 1988, issue, in which 94 percent of personnel executives felt that titles are important to employee morale. It probably still holds the same importance to workers. Although a few respondents indicated they were in favor of abolishing titles altogether, 91 percent said they would not do away with them if given the opportunity.

Neither would I. Titles provide a necessary shorthand for informing other people about what we do at our jobs. It would be awkward to have to answer the question, "What do you do at ABC Corp?" with a list of duties, instead of being able to say, "I'm vice president of operations."

Some studies have validated not only the importance of titles to employees, but also their importance to companies. Job titles often have a direct correlation with the success and growth of certain firms. When we read in newspapers and business trade magazines about a number of new executive positions being created and filled, we automatically view that company as enjoying a growth cycle. Investors respond similarly. So do potential customers who, like most of us, want to do business with companies that are solid and growing. This is distinctly psychological, of course, but what successful business hasn't benefitted from a positive psychological profile?

I believe in the judicious use of titles to motivate and retain good people, provided restraint is exercised and a department's overall balance isn't upset. One important caveat: When employees are given loftier titles *and* positions that include more responsibility, hours, and number of people for whom they are responsible—but are not given a commensurate salary increase—they have every reason to complain and to feel they've been taken advantage of. Fair is fair, regardless of whether salary caps and internal policies are involved—unless, of course, business is so bad that all salary increases are prohibited across the board.

If fairness isn't a persuasive argument, glance over at the revolving door. Armed with new and impressive titles, and angry at management, these employees will be grinding out their resumes and using their titles to find new and better-paying jobs.

Robert Half International once surveyed a cross-section of American workers for their primary reasons for seeking a job with a different company. The two major reasons were a feeling that opportunities for advancement were limited and a lack of recognition. A new and better title is certainly a legitimate form of recognition and can appease a good employee for a period of time, but it does not take the place of opportunity for legitimate advancement, including increased responsibility with matching compensation.

KNOW WHEN AN EMPLOYEE IS READY FOR A PROMOTION

Until now, I've referred to promotions, including those in title only, as a means of motivating employees when true promotional opportunities aren't available. When a position opens up, and more than one person in a department is qualified and worthy of consideration, how does a manager make that choice?

Many factors go into such a decision. But, in general, any manager might consider the following three indicators for knowing when someone is ready to move up. I call them "the ABCs of promotion."

- *Accomplishments.* There should be strong evidence that those considered for promotion have accomplished every task assigned to them over the period of their employment and also have a history of accuracy, timeliness, and creativity.
- *Boredom.* Good employees who appear to have become bored with their work, and who have demonstrated the potential for taking on greater responsibility, are prime candidates for advancement.

- *Cooperativeness.* Employees who combine professional excellence with a spirit of cooperation and team play are obviously worthy of serious consideration.

In addition, keep these thoughts in mind:

- Promote from within, if possible. This builds morale and simplifies hiring procedures. Bringing in people from the outside, unless really necessary, disrupts the team currently in place and can create an adversarial atmosphere between new boss and old guard.

- Promote only those people you feel will be good role models for other employees, as well as for new hires to be brought in at a future date. Management's decision to promote reflects on a company's reputation and can have serious morale and hiring ramifications down the road.

- Focus on professional strengths as a reason *for* promoting, rather than focusing on personal weaknesses as a reason *not* to promote. As President Harry S. Truman once said, "Never mind personal weaknesses, tell me what they can do."

Every employee has faults. However, it's important to view them within the context of a person's overall performance.

23

RAISES AND BONUSES: WHO GETS WHAT?

Rewarding Good Performance

"Enough is never enough."

The concept of giving employees a greater role in decision making and helping them feel like "partners" also encompasses the very tangible areas of raises, bonuses, and stock options. To an extent, the trend toward leaner permanent staffs, with an accompanying increase in the utilization of contract and temporary workers, has fed this movement. An increasing number of companies are reevaluating the idea of paying permanent workers set salaries based on title and job. They are exploring pay options that reward knowledge and performance. As a result, both knowledge and performance increase, which is good for any company anxious to retain the best people.

It's difficult, of course, for any company to shift gears when it comes to compensation *after* an employee has been hired at a set salary, but it can be done. Already some companies have concluded that compensation based on knowledge, performance, and overall contribution makes more sense than the present system. These forward-looking companies do not represent the majority of American business, but their efforts are being observed and analyzed by many other companies.

Judging from a recent Robert Half International survey, conducted among top executives at a cross-section of America's largest corporations, this compensation system practice will only increase. We asked them,

169

"Do you believe that variable, performance-based pay for most employees is a compensation approach that will increase, decrease, or stay the same in the next five years?" In response, 32 percent said it would increase significantly, and 47 percent said it would increase to some extent.

CONVERTING TO A PERFORMANCE-BASED PAY SYSTEM

To transition from a system of set compensation, in which pay is determined by title, to a more flexible, performance-based approach, a company must:

- Be completely certain that the new system is the result of the best available thinking

- Be satisfied that the new structure allows for equal and fair opportunity for all employees affected by the plan.

- Be prepared to sell the new concept to those whose compensation will be altered. The plan must be explained in sufficient detail—both its tangible factors and the less tangible goals it hopes to achieve. Ideally, employees will come to understand how the new system of compensation is good for them, and good for the company.

- Be committed to a sufficient amount of time for the new plan to be implemented and to prove itself.

- Create a system through which the new compensation approach can be closely monitored. At the same time, establish channels through which employees can communicate their reactions, favorable and unfavorable.

- Establish other nonfinancial means through which affected employees can gain authority. Instituting a variable, performance-based system of pay should be pointed to as but one example of the company's commitment to forging a partnership between employee and management. "We rise and fall together" is the message.

- Understand that converting from the traditional title-driven pay scale to a variable system based on knowledge and performance is a long-term approach to improving company fortunes, and that one of many benefits will be the retention of the company's best people.

Performance-based pay can go a long way toward making employees more accountable for their work, in addition to providing an attractive incentive for increased productivity. Because their extra efforts make the company more competitive in the marketplace, employees find that their own careers and jobs are strengthened, another benefit in times of employment uncertainty. As with all benefits, employees must be made aware of them. Communication should be continuing and frequent once the new system has been introduced.

Variable pay also gives employers greater control over employee compensation costs. Further, it negates the need to use promotions, raises, and bonuses as devices to sustain morale.

Identify Performance Levels that Merit Salary Increases

Naturally, any company policy, particularly one that is innovative and relatively untested, will raise questions and pose problems. With performance-based pay, the obvious question is what specific levels of performance will be considered worthy of merit increases in salary or the awarding of bonuses.

To use the analogy of professional sports, will one home run justify a raise, or will it take two, three, or four? In a service company that does not pay commissions, will bringing in six new customers be considered meritorious enough to warrant an increase in compensation, or should acquiring a dozen new accounts represent the required level of productivity?

In baseball, if hitting a home run were to be considered the most important achievement and carries with it the biggest reward, that is clearly prejudicial to pitchers, who hit few home runs.

The same problem exists in companies that have instituted performance-based pay. All participating employees must have the opportunity to reach for the stars. If those people who bring in new business receive the lion's share of increased compensation, others in positions that are less sales- and marketing-oriented will soon lose interest; the program's purpose will have been compromised.

Rewarding Team Performance. An approach some companies are taking to alleviate this fairness problem is to create teams. Instead of individuals benefitting from increased pay, the team is the recipient. This makes sense. A hot-shot salesperson might sell new accounts, but it takes back-up to service them. Everyone on a successful team—

salesperson, marketing professional, secretaries, shipping personnel, mailroom employee—shares in the nurturing of new accounts and should share in the spoils as well. An important aspect of this approach is that peer pressure encourages those employees who are not productive to pick up the pace in order to be able to participate in the rewards.

Rewarding Skills or Job Knowledge. Another approach to compensating employees by a participatory system is known as "pay-for-skills," "skill-based pay," or "knowledge-based compensation." The core of this concept is that employees are paid for how much knowledge they bring to a company, and how much additional knowledge they develop while employed (provided, of course, that they put it to good use). This isn't an entirely new concept; some factories have experimented with it for years.

Advocates of this form of pay system insist it allows for more objectivity in determining pay scales and places the emphasis on learning (which fits nicely with cross-discipline training discussed in Chapter 18). The result, they say, is a well-rounded employee who comes to know every part of the business, and who can make a greater, all-encompassing contribution. In a nutshell, the more you learn, the more you earn.

An article in the May 17, 1992, issue of *The New York Times* pointed to several companies that have implemented pay-for-skills. Quaker Oats was one of the first companies to adopt a skill-based pay scale, in the early 1970s. The participating employees were non-union factory workers at the company's pet food plant. The result reported by the company was that overall wages rose, but labor costs as a unit of output fell.

Inland Steel Bar was another company that adopted a pay-for-skills program, applying it to its unionized steel workers. It enjoyed a 15 percent gain in productivity, along with an increase in new business.

Problems with Performance-Based Pay Systems

Performance-based pay hasn't worked for every company, however. The *Times* article mentioned in the last section reported that I.D.S. Financial Services instituted such a plan in 1988 to include its back-office, mutual fund processing employees. The company said the program resulted in a division between employees who had acquired new skills and those who hadn't. As a result, I.D.S. abandoned the experiment.

Another company, which initiated a modified form of performance-based pay, established a reward system for cutting costs. The problem was that overzealous employees eliminated certain vital services and functions which, instead of cutting costs, ended up costing more.

Problems arising from new approaches to employee compensation should not be used as a rationale to dismiss the idea. Older, more entrenched systems of compensation have always had their own problems. If they hadn't, there wouldn't be the need to seek new approaches.

In many companies, raises are given across the board—a certain percentage granted to *all* employees each year. Although that formula leaves no one out, it reinforces the philosophy that *everyone* deserves a raise, even when everyone doesn't. (Of course, such raises might simply reflect cost-of-living increases. Excluding certain employees from receiving them is tantamount to a salary decrease.)

Rewarding employees whose performance has been substandard sends a clear, negative message to those who've given it their all: "It doesn't matter how much I've contributed to the company's success. We all receive a raise simply by virtue of having been there all year. Why give extra effort? The reward will be the same whether I work harder or not."

That approach to employee compensation is destined to change. Currently, companies must weather shifting economic climates, including heated-up global competition, and cannot afford to reward marginal employees, much less "carry" them for very long.

The academic world has long had a saying, "Publish or perish," which has always been viewed as a fault in the academic system. The message to today's corporate workforce must be, "Produce or perish."

Ironically, it was the former Soviet Union's Nikita Khrushchev who once nicely summed up the philosophy behind variable production-based pay. When discussing the merits of incentive programs, he said, "Call it what you will, incentives are the only way to make people work harder."

Rewarding outstanding performance, whether individual or team, with tangible increases in compensation has always been a potent incentive. However, it should be considered only one of an arsenal of ways to motivate employees.

GIVING EMPLOYEE BONUSES

Bonuses have always been a popular means of motivating employees, and undoubtedly will continue to be. Generally, they're dispensed at predetermined times of year, year's end being the most prevalent. In some cases they're based on company performance. In other cases they're not. The most popular means of determining the amount given to each employee is to base it on a percentage of salary. The bigger the salary, the bigger the bonus.

This is good. Extra cash can do wonders for employee morale, at least during the period of time it's being spent. Whether a yearly bonus carries with it lasting allegiance is conjecture.

Nonetheless, my observations of the use of employee bonuses over the years has led me to conclude that although the issuance of them is well meaning on the part of employers, they aren't always used to their best advantage. In too many instances, employees *expect* their yearly bonuses once the tradition has been established. This goes against the growing emphasis on variable, performance-based compensation. A bonus should *not* be expected each year. What should be expected is that individuals who've done a good job, singularly or as part of a team, might expect to share in the company's success in some tangible way.

Spot bonuses (as opposed to those that are regularly scheduled) can have a particularly positive impact on employees. To maximize their effectiveness, give them while deserving employees are in the midst of an especially demanding and important project, rather than waiting until it's done. Providing a second wind when the hours are long and the demands seem overwhelming is always good timing.

Another concept is to base the award on customer satisfaction. The determination is based on independent surveys of customers' attitudes towards the company. When those attitudes are positive, especially if the company ranks first, the appropriate employees are rewarded.

The Xerox Corporation uses elements of this approach in its formula for awarding bonuses. Top management decided to stop rewarding only those executives who met traditional sales and profit quotas, but also managers who rarely dealt directly with customers. Bonuses under this plan increased pay levels as much as 40 percent for those who met customer-satisfaction goals. Conversely, some lost as much as 20 percent of their total compensation if service problems plagued their areas of responsibility and were not corrected.

The bonuses awarded by Xerox are based on responses to the company's customer-satisfaction measurement survey, which is sent monthly to 40,000 customers worldwide.

AWARDING EMPLOYEE STOCK OPTIONS

Employee stock options have always been a popular tool for motivating employees. Under most plans, all eligible employees are given the option of purchasing shares of a company's stock at a future date, but at a price fixed at the time the options are granted. Having the opportunity to invest directly in a company means employees are able to invest in themselves and the fruits of their labor; the feeling of being in "partnership" with management is reinforced.

Certain groups of employees are deemed eligible to participate and are granted options to buy the stock, its value determined by the rise and fall of the market. Naturally, it behooves every employee holding shares to work hard to ensure that the company's fortunes and, by extension, their own, are enhanced. This is the motivating factor, even though few such plans have been linked to individual or team *performance*.

In a sense, traditional employee stock option plans are another *fixed* method of compensation—that is, they are not influenced by individual performance. As long as a person is in the group that is eligible to purchase stock and remains employed by the company, the option is generally available. That's why some companies are beginning to link stock option plans with performance. Like variable pay, eligibility to purchase stock is determined by individual or team achievement. The motivation is enhanced. Each employee benefits when colleagues urge them to increase productivity. Peer pressure works.

Stock option plans will undoubtedly be subject to experimentation and modification in the future, but they will remain a staple of employee motivation. A 1991 Robert Half International survey on performance-based pay asked, "How important are stock options in attracting and retaining American workers at all levels of a company?" The response: 23 percent said they are very important; 57 percent said they are somewhat important.

The major change in the way stock option plans are implemented will be, I believe, in how they are woven into a broader and more all-encompassing package of employee incentives. Performance not only will be more closely keyed to employee compensation, but also the "softer" motivations—participation in decision making, cross-discipline training, and other empowering concepts—will play an increasing role. The desired result will be empowerment programs that cover all the bases. Companies that achieve this will have developed what might be called a "victorious circle:" their employees will be motivated and loyal; the company will be known as a very good place to work; and because it is, the best available talent will seek employment there.

24

OTHER MOTIVATORS
Offering Benefits and Perks

"The ladder to success is not an escalator."

A 1992 Gallup Poll overwhelmingly pointed to good health insurance as the most important "characteristic" of any job. Although it ranks first on a list of what respondents felt were important (81 percent of them chose medical benefits), only 27 percent said they were completely satisfied with their current health insurance. This represents a sizable discrepancy between what workers say they want and what they feel they're receiving.

Other job characteristics they considered important are shown in Table 24-1, which also shows how many respondents were completely satisfied with each job characteristic.

Times have certainly changed, if this '92 Gallup poll is a barometer. It was only a few years earlier that high income would have been at the top of the list, or close to the top of any list of employee motivational factors. That's not to say that a fair and equitable wage doesn't continue to be a critically important ingredient in employee contentment. What seems to happen is that once a decent pay-line is established, other factors are allowed to loom more important.

This has been confirmed by studies Robert Half International conducted in 1992. Respondents to our questions revealed that people aren't leaving their jobs as quickly to chase after bigger money. Instead, they're leaving for such non-monetary factors such as career advancement and increased responsibility and opportunity.

176

Table 24-1   Results of 1992 Gallup Poll on Important Job Characteristics

Job Characteristic	% of Respondents who felt this job characteristic was important	% of Respondents who were completely satisfied with this job characteristic
Interesting work	78	41
Job security	78	35
Opportunity to learn new skills	68	31
Vacation of a week or more	66	35
Freedom to work independently	64	42
Recognition from co-workers	62	24
Ability to help others	58	34
Limited job stress	58	18
Regular hours	58	40
High income	56	13
Opportunities for promotion	53	20

Employers who fail to heed the inherent message in these studies—that money alone won't necessarily keep their best people—are destined to lose some of them.

OFFER FLEXIBLE BENEFITS

That health benefits rank first with employees should come as no surprise. Health care has become the dominant topic on the minds of political, economic, and business leadership. As previously pointed out, many men and women hold on to their jobs primarily to retain their company-sponsored health insurance. At the same time, employers are faced with a spiraling increase in the cost of providing these benefits to their workers and are actively seeking new approaches.

Flexible benefits programs are springing up in many American companies. In most cases, it is cost containment, rather than attempting to meet diverse employee needs that fuels this search for new ways to provide employee benefits.

Flexible benefits plans are defined as those offering employees a choice among varying types and levels of benefits. They're sometimes called "cafeteria benefits" because of the varied menu they offer. For example, employees can select a lower level of health care benefits in return for additional vacation days, or pare their life insurance benefits and opt for more extended medical coverage.

Frank DiBemardino, a Foster Higgins principal and one of the study's authors, explained, "Clearly, flex employers are making cost management a top priority in the wake of a nearly 40 percent increase in health benefit costs over the past two years.

George Faulkner, a Foster Higgins consultant and co-author of the study, commented, "The lower average cost among flex employers relates partly to the use of managed care provisions. HMOs, for example, typically adopt more competitive pricing when offered through a flexible plan."

Foster Higgins found that employers with between 2,500 and 20,000 employees have the administrative resources, budget, and staff to implement a new plan and are the most likely to offer flexible benefits.

Among industry groups, flex plans are most common with companies engaged in financial services, insurance, energy/petroleum, and education. Flex plans are less prevalent among communications, consumer product, wholesale/retail, and utility organizations, which tend to be highly unionized and which employ large numbers of part-time workers.

DEVELOP A "PARENT TRACK" FOR ADVANCEMENT

An interesting phenomenon is that during the prolonged recession at the start of the 1990s when people should have been preoccupied with holding on to their jobs, many were seeking to work less. It wasn't laziness or a lack of ambition. Rather, it was a desire to rearrange their working lives in order to have more time with family and to pursue nonvocational interests.

This movement launched the concept of parent tracking, snidely called "mommy tracking" by some because it was wrongly perceived to apply almost exclusively to women with children. *Parent tracking* is a more accurate term; the idea applies to both genders.

That workers wanted more time to spend with family prompted employers to create additional approaches to accommodate this need—flex-time, job sharing, and on-site child care among them. These, and other ideas, have been adopted in one form or another by companies across America.

Simply defined, parent tracking is a management concept that allows professional, career-oriented parents to achieve promotions within their companies, but be allowed to do so on a slower "track."

A number of large accounting firms have astutely instituted parent tracking programs in response to employee requests. Because Robert Half International deals extensively with these organizations, as well as with men and women seeking to be employed by them, I've had the chance to observe the trend closely. There's no question about it: an increasing number of candidates for employment are seeking such arrangements, and they are being accommodated in increasing numbers.

Another indicator of employees wanting to work less is the large increase in the number of men and women working in temporary capacities, rather than accepting full-time, permanent jobs. They're able to work, or to devote blocks of time to family needs.

The accounting profession is a good bellwether for parent tracking because of its traditional system of establishing paths, or tracks, to partnership status within firms. An employee who chooses parent tracking is not precluded from achieving that coveted partner plateau, but understands that it will take longer to get there, perhaps 13 or 14 years instead of nine or ten. It's a trade-off in the classic sense, one that each individual must decide to accept or decline.

From the employers' perspective, offering such flexibility requires considerable restructuring, which costs time and money. They don't do it out of altruism, but elect to offer flexible career paths and working hours because it makes good business sense. Rather than lose valuable and productive employees, they retain them while still allowing them to pursue dual goals of career success and family responsibility.

Parent tracking is more than a concept at Deloitte Touche. It's a reality. Although only female employees have chosen to participate in it thus far, it's also available to their male counterparts.

Arthur Andersen & Co. has initiated its own form of parent tracking. All men and women at the manager level are eligible. Those choosing this slower partnership track spend up to three years in the program. They work part-time and are compensated accordingly, but are included in the normal performance review process.

Because offering flexibility in its various forms to workers has become relatively commonplace in American business, Robert Half International set out in 1990 to survey workers and employers to determine their reaction to it, and the extent to which they are participating. Here are the results:

- Nearly eight out of ten men and women surveyed reported that they would sacrifice rapid career development in order to spend more time with their families. Specifically, when presented with a choice of two career paths—one with flexible full-time work hours and more family time but *slower* career advancement, the other with inflexible work hours but *faster* career advancement—78 percent chose the slower, family-oriented track.

- Two out of three said they would be willing to reduce their work hours and salaries by an average of 13 percent in order to gain family and personal time.

- A majority believe that employees who choose more flexible hours and slower career advancement ultimately will be as successful as those opting for the alternative.

- Only a third of the respondents said they would be likely to accept a promotion if it required them to spend less time with their families.

It's important to keep in mind that these surveys asked hypothetical questions. Many who embraced the concept of less work and more family time might not act on those feelings if confronted with making an actual choice in their careers.

Even with this caveat, it's clear that American business must deal with, at least, the possibility of having to restructure working conditions to meet a demand from quality employees for flexible hours.

OFFER PERSONALIZED PERKS—"LITTLE EXTRAS" THAT MEAN A LOT

The larger the employer, the more difficult it is to personalize employee benefits, but for any company seeking to motivate and retain good people, it pays to "think small" sometimes, to get to know each employee's "hot buttons" and, if possible, to offer perks that activate them.

An acquaintance of mine has two secretaries. Both are hardworking and loyal to this executive. He told me that one has a passion for seafood; the other shares her husband's love of hometown football. He doesn't have to give them sizable bonuses to keep them happy. Instead, an occasional gift certificate at the city's best seafood restaurant and tickets to a few games means more to each, respectively, than cash.

There are hundreds of small extras that cost little but can have a big impact on employee morale and productivity. In smaller companies, they can be given to individuals who are known to have a specific hot button, but in larger companies they are bunched into packages from which deserving employees can choose, based on a predetermined dollar value. Such packages can include

- The option to upgrade to first-class air travel once or twice a year for those who travel a great deal
- Being able to bring a spouse on a business trip
- Extra days off
- Gift certificates from local restaurants and stores with which the company has negotiated a lower price.
- Extra discounts on the company's products or services
- Commute-oriented packages
- Membership at a local health club
- Overnight vacation at a local inn
- Continuing education subsidy at a local college

These ideas just scratch the surface of a menu-driven system of perks. In most cases where a company wishes to provide special considerations for employees, these extras are not subject to employee choice. They're simply provided. Here are some examples:

Facilitate Commuting

A medium-sized New York publisher moved her offices from midtown Manhattan to a New Jersey suburb years ago. She was afraid she would lose a loyal corps of workers who were used to Manhattan's good restaurants, to say nothing of the convenience of walking to work. She solved it by leasing a bus to bring them to and from work each day and by establishing in the new facility a state-of-the-art kitchen where gourmet lunches were served at no charge. She didn't lose a single employee. (I'm sure there were other reasons, too, besides transportation and lunch, but those offerings certainly helped to retain these employees.)

Install an On-site Kitchen

Small improvements can always be a motivator. A municipal bond firm polls its employees and finds that most of them bring their lunch from home. What they need is a kitchen in which to heat and refrigerate the contents of their brown bags.

Hire Temporary Help When Needed

Managers at another company learn through the powerful employee grapevine that the major complaint is the reluctance of management to hire extra help during crunch times. When temporary workers are brought in, the employees feel less pressured and morale rises.

Other Ideas for Perks that Motivate

Take the time and effort to identify employee hot buttons. In most cases it costs little to satisfy employee needs, certainly a lot less than losing good people.

Although each person has specific items that are meaningful, virtually everyone responds to

- Personal notes congratulating achievements
- A few more desirable assignments
- Public recognition
- Titles
- Greeting cards and gifts for special personal occasions
- Something free such as coffee, donuts, or fruit
- A cheery, friendly work environment

ESTABLISH STRONG LEADERSHIP AND MANAGEMENT TO MOTIVATE

All things considered, one of the biggest employee motivators is *the quality and actions of management*. Free coffee and a microwave oven will never replace a management team that knows what it is doing and advances a company's goals and, by extension, the goals of its employees. Such management recognizes that enlightened leadership and employee motivation is at the crux of any company's ultimate success.

Robert Half International surveyed hundreds of executives in 1990 as to their definition of what corporate "leadership" was really all about. Fifty-three percent felt that the most important responsibility for those at the top was to motivate employees. Everyone needs and respects leadership. A company's goals necessarily must represent its employees' goals: prosperity, jobs, security, and respect.

Because the fortunes of both workers and corporate America become more inextricably intertwined as the global business climate grows increasingly complex and competitive, the partnership I speak of between employee and employer must be enhanced—and I have little doubt it will be. The "intrapreneurism of America" in which employees are less concerned about what management can *do* for them and more concerned with *the level of respect and authority* management is willing to grant them, represents the new horizon of how business will be conducted in the years ahead.

Not everyone agrees with this assessment. There's another school of thought that preaches that workers inherently want to do their best and don't need "artificial" methods to achieve it. Instead of creating awards and bonuses to inspire workers to do their jobs, advocates of this other approach urge that management get rid of the obstacles that de-motivate employees.

This approach has come to be known as "process management," based on the ideas of consultant W.E. Deming. Deming feels strongly that management should make a concerted effort to eradicate

- Thoughtless decisions
- Lack of teamwork
- Poor communication between managers and employees
- Invisible and inaccessible leadership
- Inconsistent instructions

Still, according to this article, most managers ignore Deming's advice and hold on to the following *erroneous* notions about employee motivation:

- That *positive motivational techniques* always lead to greater performance and productivity

- That *financial rewards* are a foolproof motivator
- That some employees *don't need* motivation
- That *fear* is the best way to motivate most workers
- That a happy worker is *always* a productive worker
- That workers today are *less* motivated than they were in the past

Whether employee motivation and empowerment is a matter of removing obstacles or injecting positive programs of new incentives—more likely it's a reasoned combination of both—the salient fact shouts loud and clear. Employees cannot and must not be taken for granted. Every company's future fortunes depend on its workers. A trite statement perhaps, but one that unfortunately seems to elude too many executives whose companies, and own careers, might well rest on their eventual acceptance of it.

25

OUT OF SIGHT, OUT OF MIND?

Motivating Transferred Employees

"Employee transfers are a 'moving' experience."

Employees who work for companies with far-flung operations are sometimes faced with a perplexing decision—whether to accept or decline a transfer to another location. The difficulties of relocation don't fall entirely on the shoulders of affected employees. Management, too, assumes an additional challenge when it relocates a good person. Two critically important questions that need to be answered are

- What steps will be taken to ease the employee's transition to a new place and situation?
- How will that person continue to be motivated when he or she is far from corporate "home?"

Employees whose work at headquarters has been exemplary enough to warrant transfer to responsible positions elsewhere deserve to have their transfers handled well. Otherwise, employers risk losing good people. It isn't enough to pay all the expenses inherent in a move. That's a given, and should be considered only one of many motivating factors, just as salary and benefits in general are but two factors in the arsenal of motivational tools. It's the extra things that can make the difference between a happily transferred person and one who becomes disillusioned and discontented.

What a company is willing to do for a relocated employee is highly individual and depends on a variety of circumstances. If there is one concept that should be applied to every case, it's the need to *be sensitive to the stress* that is inherent in relocating, stress that touches everyone involved. Moving is disruptive and traumatic for employee and family alike. Anticipating this additional pressure and doing whatever possible to alleviate it helps ensure a successful relocation.

RELOCATING TRANSFERRED EMPLOYEES

Before examining the intangible factors that go into building the morale of a transferred worker, let's take a look at the nuts and bolts of relocation, not in dollar figures but in the way it's handled.

Companies that routinely transfer employees usually have a formal structure through which to smooth the process. Issues addressed in these policies are

- Helping transferred employees sell their homes. What help is the employer prepared to give in this regard? Policies vary from company to company. Many will assist in the sale of an employee's current home, or will make provisions to guarantee its fair market value should the employee be unable to sell it before leaving. Will real estate fees and administrative expenses associated with selling a house be covered? If an employee's home is sold, but that individual intends to rent in the new location, will the employer make provisions to help offset the impact of capital gains?

- Helping the transferred employee break a lease. If the employee is renting a home and must break a lease in order to relocate, some companies agree to cover the loss of security payments or other expenses resulting from such action.

- Helping transferred employees with temporary living expenses. To what extent will the employer pick up expenses during the transitional period between the employee leaving his or her current residence and finding a new home? Will a temporary living allowance be advanced to cover such expenses as hotel or short-term apartment rental, per diem allowances for meals, vehicle rental, and other costs the employee and family will incur?

Job transfers often involve a better title, salary, and enhanced career potential. However, if those positive factors are mitigated by losses pertaining the employee's home, the bloom could come quickly off the rose for this otherwise motivated individual.

Some companies create a thoughtful and comprehensive system to ease the transfer of employees away from headquarters, but fail to plan for their eventual return. Every company that relocates employees should have a formalized "repatriation" policy that is adequately explained before employees relocate. Will the company cover all expenses related to returning to home base? Under what circumstances will the company *not* assume the expense of bringing back an employee?

To prepare, companies should establish a policy that covers the possibility of transferred employees choosing to resign while in their new location to take a job with another firm. Will they be expected to pay back a portion, or all, of the relocation expenses paid by the employer that sent them there? What about employees who are fired while in their new domain? Will the company pay to return them to their home cities?

TRANSFERRING EMPLOYEES OVERSEAS— SUCCESSFULLY

I used the term *repatriation*, which is generally reserved for when an individual returns from a foreign land. This might be a good time to comment on the special challenge of relocating employees overseas.

Any relocation, domestic or foreign, poses problems, but they're necessarily more complex when sending employees to foreign countries. Here are just a few potential difficulties:

- Language—The adjustment for employees and their families is compounded by different languages, cultures, and a variety of other factors.

- Taxes—There can be significant tax problems if employees must pay taxes to the host country. In some extreme cases, taxes can be greater than the employees' base salaries!

- Business etiquette—There is the need to acclimate to a different way of doing business, based on local protocol.

- Education—The right education for employees' children must be established to ensure they haven't "lost ground" on returning home.

- Spouse assimilation—The employees' spouses face the challenge of making new friends, assimilating into a foreign culture, and perhaps finding work.

Employees and their families face these problems no matter where they move, but overseas assignments intensify them for both employees and employers. Companies doing business abroad must hire men and women whose credentials include the ability and aptitude to function in a foreign environment. These are special people, often with special credentials. To lose even one because steps weren't taken to avoid it puts a severe crimp in a company's staffing and competitive position, especially if the employee goes to work for a competitor.

A final point: no matter what agreements concerning benefits and compensation are struck between employers and relocating employees, put them in writing. It doesn't have to be a formal contract, but a simple letter, understood and agreed to by both parties, can head off those sticky situations where employees and their families, already moved and settled in a new country, call and say, "But I thought you said you would give me. . . ."

RELOCATING SPOUSES OR "SIGNIFICANT OTHERS"

In this age of dual breadwinners, the relocation of an employee must take into consideration the spouse's job, not only because that person might be reluctant to abandon a fulfilling career, but because of financial requirements. In 1989, *Personnel Administration* projected that approximately 60 percent of all couples who relocated relied on two incomes to sustain their quality of life. I believe that it's much higher today.

Losing a second income, even if the relocation carries with it a raise, can seriously impact a family's financial stability. That's why many companies find it difficult to convince an employee to move unless the working needs of the spouse or partner are addressed.

The two-income family isn't the only societal change to which companies must adapt when transferring employees. The definition of "spouse" has expanded to include other than the traditional husband and wife. Because employees are "single" doesn't mean that significant people don't exist in their lives, perhaps significant enough to keep them from accepting a transfer to another location unless those persons accompany them at company expense. The debate whether to include these "significant others" in the package of benefits accompanying employee relocation is the same one many companies face concerning the inclusion of non-married individuals on benefit plans.

It's a policy decision that must fit comfortably within each employer's philosophy of benefits. Either way, it's an issue that is with us and cannot be ignored when structuring relocation policies.

MOTIVATING TRANSFERRED EMPLOYEES

Assuming all the tangibles of relocating employees have been satisfactorily resolved, the need to motivate them in their new assignments takes centerstage. Many techniques apply, whether employees work at the home office or are thousands of miles away; distance only amplifies the difficulties.

The psyche of employees working far from the company's core of operations can change, especially if the company's fortunes have slipped. When that happens, there is increased apprehension about the future, fueled by a grapevine that often fails to get things right. A feeling of isolation sets in which, if allowed to fester, can turn into paranoia that gets in the way of job performance.

Employees should be given a clear understanding of their career path opportunities within the company before being asked to make the decision to accept new assignments. That understanding should be reinforced throughout the employee's tour of duty. Consistent and frequent contact and communication is the key to accomplishing this.

Keep Transferred Employees Informed of the Company's Future Business Plans

Because relocated employees no longer enjoy the same level and frequency of contact with departments in the home corporate offices, nor the frequency of personal contact with superiors in their chain of command, keeping them informed of corporate planning provides them with a benchmark for how their progress will be evaluated. In addition, it makes them feel part of the team and its goals, an important morale builder.

To further this goal, there's another step to take. In addition to informing relocated employees of corporate planning, invite their input, even though they no longer routinely attend meetings at headquarters. Distance should not diminish an employee's worth when it comes to new ideas. After all, they will be the ones called on to translate future plans into action. Failing to seek their views potentially sends a signal that they don't count anymore. Even if their ideas are not put into play, they've at least received the message that they still matter and are as important as those closest to the corporate center.

Keep Transferred Employees Informed of Their Career Opportunities Within the Company

Employees working in distant locations often suffer the fear that when promotion and assignment opportunities open up, those closest to the seat of power will have the inside track by virtue of their being able to nurture useful intracompany relationships at higher echelons. "Out of sight, out of mind" looms large.

Such fears and apprehensions are exacerbated when headquarters issues missives announcing new directions or projects that seem to come out of the blue. Seeking the views of employees in satellite offices at the earliest stages goes a long way toward heading off this apprehension. Naturally, many corporate plans cannot be shared with the rank-and-file until the time is right. However, too often, the right time passes simply because those doing the planning aren't factoring in the potential impact on employee morale, especially for those whose faces are no longer seen on a regular basis.

HOW TO COMMUNICATE WITH OFFSITE EMPLOYEES

Communicating with employees in distant operations can utilize already existing employee channels, including company publications. Those at headquarters know what's going on by virtue of being close to the action; not so with men and women working out in the field. For them, employee publications can be a lifeline to home. These publications provide:

- Information about what others are doing at headquarters
- A format through which to highlight, for the rest of the company, how branch offices and facilities are faring
- A sense of corporate strategy, goals, and activities that have bearing on their lives and careers

It's always difficult to maintain a proper balance, using, for example, an eight-page monthly employee newsletter, between corporate news and the activities of employees in satellite locations. (The better publications accomplish this, however.) Even when there is that proper balance in well-crafted employee publications, there usually isn't sufficient room to detail all the important corporate news that employees in the field want and need to know.

Faced with this, a number of companies have launched management newsletters as adjuncts to monthly employee newspapers. Information contained in them is reserved for topics of high-level corporate activities, information that is important for all employees, especially those not privy to word-of-mouth channels that carry such news through the halls of headquarters, often before it's announced.

The extent to which an employer will go to satisfy the distant employees' natural craving for corporate news depends on philosophy, priorities, and, of course, budget. Some go to great lengths to keep the "troops" informed, including the use of audio and video reports, regularly scheduled satellite telecommunications conferences, and daily management "newswires." Others do considerably less and hope for the best.

No matter how extensive the network of communications tools utilized by management to keep in touch, nothing has greater impact than personal contact. That's easy when employees are down the hall or on the other side of the building. It's significantly more complex when they're in a different city or country.

For the most part, top levels of management seem to maintain closer personal contact with employees in the field than do managers lower on the chain of command. This is due primarily to the role top executives are expected to play. Frequent visits to all company operations allows them not only to take the pulse of outlying offices and factories, but also to boost morale by their arrival at those facilities. We look up to our leaders, wanting them to be slightly larger than life. When they take the time to shake our hands, we're flattered and buoyed.

More frequent contact between employees in distant locations and their *immediate superiors* can have even greater meaning, and produce more immediate results. Obviously, budgets play a role in how often line managers can travel, but the more visits to subordinates in faraway places, the better. Visiting line managers have more time to spend with their subordinates, time in which to expound new company developments, operating changes, and the activities of colleagues in other offices.

For managers who hit the road with frequency, they develop a better feel for how things are going outside their offices at headquarters. All of the questions their subordinates have about the company's goals, and their fit into achieving them, can be answered directly, something no publication can accomplish.

No matter the mix of communications approaches—employee newsletters, management newsletters, daily dispatches, and personal visits—the goal is to head off a sense of corporate isolation in non-headquarters personnel. It may take time and effort to achieve this, but retaining these people and keeping them motivated seems to be worth every cent and minute.

Many people hang favorite sayings above their desks to remind them of important concepts: "The buck stops here;" "Think;" "Smile;" and countless others. I propose that every employer hang a sign that reads: "Remember the workers." If that slogan were heeded by more employers when making decisions, morale automatically would become less of a problem for everyone, whether nearby or far away.

26

STRESS = BURNOUT

Reducing Employee Stress

"A little stress brings out the best; A lot of stress brings out the worst."

"Stressed out." "Strung out." "Burned out." Or as they used to say, a "nervous breakdown."

Any worker in the current business climate, with its mergers, acquisitions, LBOs, and downsizing, knows first-hand that stress has increased in the workplace. Jobs are not as secure as they once were, and most companies are calling on staffs to accomplish more with fewer people. Hours are longer; raises and bonuses are smaller. At the same time, the pressures of daily living seem to have intensified. All of which translates into more stress, on more people.

Levels of employee stress are too intangible to measure accurately, but some attempts have been made. A recent Gallup survey, sponsored by the New York Business Group on Health, asked medical directors and personnel directors to evaluate the extent of the problem. Almost three-quarters of those responding considered stress to be a pervasive problem in the workplace, and they pointed to lost productivity as the major consequence.

Any manager concerned with sustaining employee morale and with motivating and retaining good people must, of necessity, be sensitive to stress levels. Unfortunately, because most managers are under increased stress themselves, they often fail to acknowledge the problems stress causes in their staffs. "Grin and bear it," is how they sum it up. "We're *all* under stress, so stop complaining."

That's not good enough, nor does it make any sense. If employees are called on to do more with less because of downsizing, but their productivity levels are lower due to stress, less work will get done. If corporate and departmental goals are to be achieved, the negative impact of stress must be addressed by everyone.

RECOGNIZE WHEN STRESS BECOMES BURNOUT

Burnout is a term more commonly used in the business world than *stress*, but the terms aren't interchangeable. Stress is a condition we experience every day. Burnout, at least as it is popularly defined, results when stress levels become too high. In other words, there is a cause-and-effect relationship between stress and burnout.

An employee is thought to be burned out when the spark is gone, when there is little motivation to excel or even to perform routine tasks up to previously accepted levels. Caring ceases. Goals become meaningless. challenges are no longer met with enthusiasm. In general, the employee has run out of coping skills.

The medical profession has identified a set of symptoms that herald the onset of employee burnout:

- Excessive fatigue
- Headache
- Gastrointestinal problems
- Sleep disorders

Management has its own signals that an employee has burned out, or is close to burnout:

- Lack of motivation
- Pronounced negativity
- Lack of creativity
- High absenteeism

There are undoubtedly many other signs and symptoms that point to an employee feeling burned out. In my experience, there is one overriding tip-off that it's time to pay attention to individuals whose performance has slipped: when employees begin to feel, and express, the belief that they are giving more than they are receiving.

RECOGNIZE WHEN STRESS IS SHORT-TERM FATIGUE

No one, including myself, would debate that some employees can become "burned out" after prolonged periods of stressful deadlines and workloads. It's bound to happen. However, at the risk of sounding like one of those callous managers mentioned earlier, I do question the extent of it.

Invariably, when a concept like burnout becomes popular and slips into the language, there will be those who adopt it too quickly, that is, when it is being applied inappropriately. Suffering fatigue after a long, hard project that demanded many extra hours of concentration is normal and natural. Does this truly represent burnout? Has the fire really been extinguished in those men and women who saw the project through to a successful conclusion, or will a good night's sleep or perhaps a long weekend away put things right?

PREVENTING EXTREME STRESS

No matter what it's called, undue stress does take its toll on employee productivity, and astute managers will keep their stress-antennas extended to gauge its level.

Some stress is not only normal, it's beneficial. It keeps us sharp and focused. Absence of at least some stress can cause us to become lethargic and to lose motivation.

When stress impacts negatively on productivity, it's time to take action. Some companies spend millions on wellness programs, including in-house counseling. Others team up with local gyms and offer employees discounted membership rates, or conduct on-site exercise classes during the workday. This is all to the good.

Even in such forward-looking companies, managers can go even further in helping combat stress and boost productivity. A workout in a gym might benefit some individuals, but not everyone. Returning to that hot-button approach outlined in Chapter 24, getting to know *what causes stress* in each individual employee and taking steps to alleviate it on a case-by-case basis can reap rewards. Other ideas include the following:

- Provide a few helping hands when the workload is overwhelming.
- Acknowledge the stress an employee is experiencing, and praise that person (often) for doing such a good job under difficult circumstances.

- Know when a long, leisurely lunch is due to break the tension, or an extra day or few hours off.
- Be sensitive to family pressures. An employee under stress often carries it home to the family. Long hours away from home create additional pressure. Drop the family a personal note acknowledging the strain everyone has been under, and thank family members for being understanding and supportive.
- Pitch in. Tough projects are resented less when the boss rolls up the sleeves and lends a hand.
- Always encourage a sense of humor. Nothing takes the edge off a difficult task better than a few hearty laughs.

One key to reducing stress levels is to apply as much organization and order as possible to tasks. This includes clearly defining each employee's goal.

We've all experienced it: faced with multiple projects and without a clear sense of what is to be accomplished, and in what order, the amount appears to be overwhelming. We work at one project, do a little on another, start a third. None is completed. *It* is still overwhelming.

Good managers will recognize when this stage has been reached and will call in the employee to discuss breaking down an overwhelming task into individual components. Such a meeting is an excellent opportunity to include the employee in planning as well, and is a way to communicate the value and esteem in which a supervisor holds his or her people. Ask employees the following questions:

- What do you think should take priority?
- Will completing one job make working on the next one easier?
- What problems need to be solved?
- What are the roadblocks to timely completion?
- What additional support is needed?

Usually, the people actually doing a job have a better handle on how to get it done than does a supervisor, especially in a large department when many projects are simultaneously underway. Give employees as much leeway as possible. Unless their decisions conflict with overall department and company goals, they'll work more efficiently and with less stress when they have a clear picture of where they're going and what's expected of them.

27

"I QUIT"

Dealing with Good People Who Resign

"Quitting a job is better than quitting on a job."

No matter how close to perfection a company has come in its hiring and retention programs—competitive salaries, solid benefits package, stimulating working conditions, respect for each individual employee, fair and equitable promotion policies, ongoing training, *everything* to provide a productive, satisfying job environment—there will be employees who will resign. In many cases, it will come as a surprise to the employer. In others, employees will have exhibited telltale signs that all is not well and that they're poised to leave. Picking up on these signals early enables an employer to take steps to head off a resignation, depending, of course, on why the employee has decided to leave and whether making such an attempt is in the employer's best interest.

RECOGNIZE WHEN AN EMPLOYEE IS DISSATISFIED

Some of the more obvious signs of employee restlessness are

- A noticeable change in attitude, particularly when it shifts from active and involved to passive and uncaring. Employees seriously looking for another job tend to pull back in their level of involvement, especially with long-range projects and planning.

- Less communication with management. Individuals engaged in a job search usually try to minimize contact with their bosses to avoid awkward conversations. In a sense, they attempt to become "invisible," which, of course, only increases their visibility to an astute manager.

- Longer lunch hours. This, like many signs of pending departure, becomes more obvious if patterns are broken. Employees whose jobs routinely allow for long lunches won't be as noticed as those who generally grab a quick sandwich and spend the rest of lunch reading, or those who bring lunch to work with them.

- An abrupt increase in absences, sick days, and time off during the workday for medical appointments. (Bear in mind that there could be a need to visit doctors and dentists more frequently for legitimate reasons.)

- A change in vacation plans. Employees who want to devote full-time to a job search often ask that their vacations be rescheduled. Others, already hired and ready to announce their departure, might wish to get in a vacation before starting new jobs.

- A marked increase in the number of personal phone calls made and received. Most prospective employers will not call a candidate at his or her current place of employment, but some will, using false names and reasons for calling. Often, spouses are the conduit through which dates and times of interviews are transmitted.

- A noticeable change in grooming and dress.

- A neater desk, particularly when personal mementos begin to vanish. On the other hand, if the desk has always been neat but is now piled with papers, it could mean the employee is getting ready to leave and is no longer concerned about neatness.

- When an employee known to take work home each evening stops doing it. The individual no longer seeks the benefits that working at home produces.

- Resumes inadvertently left in a copy or fax machine and discovered by a supervisor. There's also word-of-mouth. Members of an employer's professional network of colleagues are often aware that a valuable employee has been looking for a new job. Keeping eyes and ears open for such "evidence" can be helpful, provided it doesn't become a paranoid obsession.

WHY DO PEOPLE QUIT THEIR JOBS?

There are as many answers to this question as there are people, ranging from purely personal needs to career opportunities, from personality conflicts to better salaries and loftier titles.

Robert Half International commissioned a nationwide survey of leading corporations in 1988 to better understand why employees pick up and leave, and I believe the results are still applicable today. This question was asked of employers: Why did they think good and valuable employees leave their jobs? (Responses were based, to some extent, on exit interviews.) The majority (seven of ten) felt it was because employees either did not believe they'd received enough recognition for their good work, or perceived their opportunities for advancement as too limited.

Here's how the responses broke down:

- Limited opportunities for advancement: 47 percent.
- Lack of recognition: 26 percent.
- Unhappiness with management: 15 percent.
- Inadequate salary or benefits: six percent.
- Bored with the job: six percent.

FIND OUT IF AN EMPLOYEE IS JOB HUNTING

Knowing ahead of time that a valued employee is thinking of looking elsewhere or has already begun the process gives an employer crucially important time to react. Once an individual has accepted another job and resigns, the current employer's hands are tied. Yes, a counteroffer can be made in an attempt to change the employee's mind, but this seldom works. Even when it does, it doesn't work for very long. Employees who decide to stay because the pot has been sweetened are usually gone within a year anyway.

Once an employer decides that an employee intends to leave, it's best to confront that person directly: "Are you planning on leaving us?" Most people, when asked such a question, will find it difficult to lie. If they do, the lie is generally transparent.

It's important for a number of reasons to ascertain whether an employee is job hunting:

- Most employees will give adequate notice, but some won't. The more lead time an employer has to consider restaffing, the better.

- Having the opportunity to discuss why an employee wishes to leave can provide insight into what problems exist within a department. This can also be accomplished during a formal exit interview, but the earlier such conversations take place, the more time is available for corrective action.

- If the employee is especially valuable to the department and company, the chances of retaining that person are enhanced if the attempt is made *before* he or she has accepted another position. As mentioned earlier, extending a counteroffer after the fact is generally a wasted exercise, since that person, in all likelihood, will be gone within a year. In addition, word of the counteroffer may get around to other employees and tempt them to threaten leaving in the hope of receiving a raise as inducement to stay.

- If, on the other hand, the employer is not sorry to see the employee resign, the opportunity exists to ask the individual to depart immediately (with separation payment according to company practice). Employees who conduct a job search on company time do that company little good. Colleagues usually end up having to assume extra work while the employee looks for a new job. Also, because word that the employee is looking will undoubtedly sneak into the grapevine, morale can suffer.

HOW TO KEEP AN EMPLOYEE FROM RESIGNING

Although topping a financial offer made by another employer seldom results in long-term retention, there are things that can be considered in lieu of money that could serve to keep a good employee from leaving, depending on the reasons that person is looking elsewhere.

As the survey cited earlier in this chapter clearly indicated, most employees leave in search of opportunity for advancement and greater recognition. If one of these problems exists, look for ways to place the individual in charge of special projects or a newly formed task force or committee designed to attack a pervasive problem.

Be creative. Tap into those employee hot-buttons. If continuing education emerges from conversations as especially important, find the funds to pay for it. You'll end up with a better informed and trained worker. To increase recognition, reassign offices so that the employee ends up with a nicer one. To improve the variety of assignments and provide a stimulus, send the individual on trips to satellite operations.

Taking steps such as these accomplishes something worthwhile, whether or not they succeed in keeping the person. If the employee decides to stay, the mission has been accomplished. If the employee still decides to leave, the employer has established a reputation as caring and sensitive. As a result, the departing employee not only will have good things to say about the former employer to new colleagues, but also might be more inclined to return at some future date. Always leave the door open for good people to get back in touch. Things may not work out with the new job, and if they do, former employees can become excellent sources of referrals.

A few words about formal exit interviews. First, a caveat: never conduct exit interviews with employees who were fired. They're usually angry, and their comments are likely to be warped and unreliable.

Second, if communication between departing employee and superiors has been good over the course of employment, chances are that more valuable information already will have been obtained than an exit interview will uncover, but conduct one anyway, preferably with the highest level manager who had contact with the employee. Encourage candor. Give the employee a sense that his or her thoughts and suggestions are still valuable.

Every employer is unhappy when a top-notch employee leaves. If motivational and retention programs have been in place and carried out, fewer people will resign. However, some will, no matter what. When that happens, celebrate the years of solid and productive work provided by the employee, part on a positive note, and keep in touch.

28

THE TORTURE OF FIRE

Handling That Unpleasant Chore of Firing Someone

"The more right people hired, the fewer wrong people fired."

There are three simple truths about firing:

1. Most employees lose their jobs long before they are actually fired.
2. Most employees know they're going to be fired long before it actually happens and believe (down deep) that they deserve it.
3. If most employees don't know they're in danger of being fired long before it actually happens, management hasn't done its job.

Being dismissed from a job is never pleasant for the employee. In the majority of cases, it isn't pleasant for the employer, who is faced with breaking the bad news to fellow human beings that their services are no longer needed—or worse, no longer desired. Of course, there are some employees whose performance, attitude, and general presence is so disruptive and distasteful that telling them to leave is more a relief than an unwelcome task. Those situations, however, are relatively rare.

Be that as it may, having to dismiss employees for cause is an integral responsibility of management. Not everyone who is hired works out. Even if considerable care is taken to evaluate resumes, conduct effective, revealing interviews, and check those all-important references, circumstances and people change over time.

As much of a "science" as hiring can ever be, it will always pose a risk factor. In some situations, the "perfect candidate" proves to be not so perfect. Thomas Edison was fired from his job with a railroad for setting a baggage car ablaze while conducting an experiment. Henry Ford felt it necessary to fire Lee Iacocca. Warner Brothers fired former President Ronald Reagan when he was a motion picture actor.

WHY EMPLOYEES ARE FIRED

There are many reasons to fire someone, but most fall into one of four categories:

- Failure to perform. This may be defined in many ways but usually involves incompetence or unwillingness to do the job as it's supposed to be done.
- Insubordination. Habitual disregard of company rules is certainly grounds for dismissal, and may include lying or discriminatory treatment of subordinates.
- Reduction of the work force. This is sometimes unavoidable, depending on the business climate.
- Embezzlement, fraud, or other crimes. This can include a cornucopia of offenses against the company, including activities that represent a conflict of interest.

A survey conducted by Robert Half International explored many more reasons than these four. The 1988 poll found that while incompetence was the leading cause cited by employers for dismissing employees, other reasons also came into play. Except for "mega"-layoffs, the reasons are still true today. Vice-presidents and personnel directors from America's 1,000 largest companies were asked: "What is the single greatest reason for firing an employee?" The results broke down in the following order:

- Incompetence: 39 percent
- Inability to get along with others: 17 percent
- Dishonesty or lying: 12 percent
- Negative attitude: 10 percent
- Lack of motivation: 7 percent
- Failure or refusal to follow instructions: 7 percent
- All other reasons: 8 percent

That so many employers point to incompetence says something, I believe, about how lax some companies are when hiring. After all, hiring boils down to choosing individuals to do specific jobs, jobs they presumably are equipped to handle. If they're dismissed for "incompetence," they evidently weren't qualified from the outset, and shouldn't have been hired. Why were they? Hiring managers should ask themselves these questions:

- Were claims of their education, technical knowledge, and experience exaggerated?
- Did they do too good a job of selling themselves during interviews, glossing over technical questions?
- Did their references fudge the truth?
- Were references adequately checked?
- Were references checked at all?
- Did the employer somehow not follow all the proper procedures in the hiring process, such as detailing needed skills in a job description?

There will always be a certain number of people who'll slip past even the most stringent employer scrutiny. The fewer the better. Remember: The more right people hired, the fewer "wrong" people fired.

AVOID FIRING EMPLOYEES BY HIRING THE RIGHT EMPLOYEES

Hiring begins, of course, with a thorough review of corporate staffing and employment procedures, including a hard-nosed look at job specifications. Many instances of so-called incompetence result from having poorly defined the job to be filled, or even changing the definition after someone has filled it.

Once a job has been adequately defined and the technical qualifications to perform it have been *realistically* established, the entire process of hiring—finding candidates through personnel recruiters, advertising, networking, evaluating resumes, interviewing, and reference checking—should be analyzed. It's expensive for an employer to make hiring mistakes that lead to the need to repeatedly fire and hire, to say nothing of the emotional toll on employer and employees alike. Any extra time and effort spent in hiring properly is worth the investment.

Yet, when an employee hasn't worked out for whatever reason, it's incumbent on management to dismiss that person for the company's good, and often for the employee's own good as well. (A person in an unrealistic situation will only become disheartened and discouraged.) Mediocrity dominates in too many firms because supervisors either haven't established a workable system of identifying nonproductive and disruptive workers or haven't developed the resolve to fire them. When this situation is allowed to exist, everyone suffers—the employee who keeps the job but never advances; valuable co-workers who become disenchanted and leave; and, of course, the department, the division, and the entire company.

Management-by-Fear

Under most circumstances, management-by-fear not only creates an unpleasant working environment, but also inspires no self-generated productivity and pride in performance. On the other hand, a *reasonable* fear of being fired can be a positive motivator for employees who have been warned repeatedly that they are not performing up to expectation.

No one wants to be fired, especially from a good job. It's a blow to an individual's pride as well as to his or her financial security. But in some instances, the fear of being fired is so great that it gets in the way of individual achievement and leads to employees deliberately choosing to be "underemployed."

I once worked with a young man who deliberately sought jobs that paid far less than he was worth. When I asked him about it, he told me that if he were paid less, his chances of being dismissed were less. He never took any risks in the jobs he'd held, content to maintain a low profile and to toil quietly in the background. He was paralyzed by fear of losing a job, and he's not an aberration. There are many men and women who approach their careers in the same manner.

This breed of worker aside, a healthy fear of losing a job can be positive for employees and their employers, provided it's based on standards and expectations set by an employer that are realistic and fair to all and that are clearly and adequately communicated to every employee.

LAY THE GROUNDWORK BEFORE FIRING

Before examining effective ways to dismiss a nonproductive employee, let's review how to lay the supporting groundwork to be fair to both employee and employer when a firing becomes necessary. Here are some guidelines:

- Formalize what constitutes grounds for dismissal, clearly communicate them at the outset of each employee's hiring.

- Never promise job security and be certain your employee handbook doesn't read like an employment contract.

- Keep careful records of all unsatisfactory work performance and conduct. Before discharging any employee, give and document ample and prior warnings of dissatisfaction—in writing.

- Conduct regular performance reviews, and maintain records of all reviews in the event a firing decision must be defended.

- Consider the more frequent use of employment contracts, which, among other things, spell out conditions under which an employer may dismiss an employee.

- Have your legal counsel regularly review *all* written materials that bear on the rules, regulations, and conditions of the employer-employee relationship. In most instances, run the details of any firing past a company lawyer.

In addition to these guidelines, the following advice can be useful when the firing of employees becomes necessary. They might be called the "never rules":

- Never fire in anger; it only makes an unpleasant situation worse. In addition, words said in anger may be used later by a dismissed employee to try to prove personal animosity on the part of an employer.

- Never fire before exhausting all prospects for communication. If the urge to fire is caused by a specific, isolated problem, level with the employee and get his or her recommendations for avoiding a repetition.

- Never fail to consider the possibility that a personality conflict, however subtle, might be behind a decision to fire an employee. If the reason for dismissal doesn't clearly fall into one of the three basic categories listed earlier in this chapter, such a personal conflict could be at play. If so, consider alternatives, including a transfer.

- Never fire a valuable employee whose work has begun to suffer because of emotional or psychological problems until an attempt has been made to seek professional help for that person. Reaching out to a talented, productive employee in his or her time of personal travail can salvage a good person. If the employee has close, caring friends in the company, seek their counsel on how to return the troubled person to productive status. There's a slight potential risk that the troubled employee will be offended, but that may be the best method to help this person.

HOW TO FIRE AN EMPLOYEE GRACEFULLY AND PROFESSIONALLY

When all attempts to avoid dismissing an employee have failed and the decision has been made to sever the relationship, the "nasty task" of actually doing the firing must fall to someone. There aren't any painless ways to fire a person, but there are certain standards to which all employers should adhere.

It should be done by the employee's immediate supervisor. Alternatively, it could be done by the highest ranking person in the company to whom the employee is accustomed to talking during the course of a normal business day. Delegating the firing authority to another person in order to avoid personal discomfort is wrong. In addition, an employee should never be fired by someone of equal rank.

The employee should be treated with respect. Every person, even one who has proved to be a bad and nettlesome employee, deserves respect as a human being and should be allowed to maintain his or her dignity at what is a distinctly undignified time. If possible, ask the employee to leave the same day he or she is informed about the separation. There are several reasons for attempting this. Being allowed, or even encouraged, to hang around only embarrasses the individual and may unsettle and disturb others in the organization. Also, in most cases, the discharged employee should not meet with the person hired as a replacement.

Firing should be done in private and in person. It should never be done over the phone, via computer voice mail, by mail, or at a meal. As mentioned, it's usually best handled by the employee's immediate supervisor, provided that person knows how to best protect the company.

The employee should be given all information relevant to termination. Be direct at the start of the conversation: "Jim, we're going to ask you to leave." Then, make the reasons for the decision to dismiss the individual clear, using documentation where necessary to substantiate those reasons. Spell out the terms of severance, including pay, continuing benefits to which the employee will be eligible, details of any pension of profit-sharing money that might be payable, and provide information about insurance. Although many of these details may be handled in-depth by a human resources department, the person doing the actual firing should have general knowledge of company policy and the dismissed individual's personal situation.

The firing should be handled gently. Always use words other than "fired." It's too harsh a term. A few gentler substitutions are dismiss, terminate, discharge, outplace, let go.

The employer should be prepared for an angry, bitter, sometimes vehement response or tears from the dismissed employee. In either case, don't allow yourself to be drawn into an acrimonious conversation. If an employee demonstrates such responses, it's best to ask that person to vacate the premises immediately.

The employer may need to discuss the firing with other employees. If it's obvious to the person doing the firing that the employee will twist the reasons for having been dismissed, communicate to concerned others in the company the true reason for the action's having been taken. In the event such action is deemed necessary, the information should be painstakingly accurate and be communicated clearly, with all comments kept on a strictly professional level. Derogatory personal comments about departing employees not only are inappropriate, but also could come back to haunt a company should a dismissed employee take legal action.

The employer may want to offer outplacement services. Employees who react more rationally to being dismissed and who've been let go for reasons other than malfeasance or lack of performance might be deserving of certain courtesies to ease their job search. The use of an office and equipment, telephone, outplacement services, and other aids not only helps a departing employee, it creates an amicable situation that could prove mutually beneficial in the future.

We've all known employers who, rather than fire an employee, prefer to make the work situation sufficiently unpleasant to force a resignation. The employee is demoted, relieved of interesting assignments, given a reduced bonus, assigned to a smaller office, and, in general, kept out of the mainstream of company activity.

This approach not only strips away any remaining pride from the employee, it sabotages the company's morale and resulting productivity. I strongly reject it as a viable method for dealing with employees who are no longer in favor. A company should treat all its employees with respect, regardless of the circumstances.

Finally, use the firing of an employee as a reason for analyzing what went wrong, especially if you were the one who did the actual firing. It's very easy for top management to blame the departed employee's immediate supervisor for creating the situation leading to the dismissal.

Of course, it's also a good time for everyone who had been involved in hiring the individual to take a second look at the entire process. If employers don't continually learn from their mistakes, they are doomed to repeat them—hardly an original saying but one that has considerable validity.

29

IN SUMMARY

A Checklist of Ideas on Hiring and Keeping the Best Employees

"Good ideas breed good ideas."

There can be no end to the quest by employers to stop (or at least to slow down) their revolving doors through which good employees come and go. The task is simply too critical to competitive business. To slow the movement of the door, every employer concerned with the cost and turmoil of frequent staff changes must constantly seek new and better ways to choose and hire good people, and to keep them. It doesn't automatically happen. There are no shortcuts to help companies find and retain quality candidates. It takes planning, commitment, and hard work.

This chapter summarizes some highlights and thoughts. It's a checklist of sorts. I'm a believer in checklists and use them in virtually every aspect of my life. If veteran airline pilots with thousands of hours of experience consult a checklist every time they fly, I figure one can help me, too.

If you aren't a believer in making lists as memory joggers, then view this chapter as a simple reminder that retaining good people demands hiring smart in the first place, the implementation of tried-and-true practices, and, above all, the determination to make it work.

SIX WAYS TO FIND GOOD EMPLOYEES

1. Seek personal recommendations. Ask present employees, former employees, and business associates for referrals. Remember to be cautious. No matter what the source of a candidate, check references thoroughly. Don't "pre-hire."

2. Recruit from within. The best candidate for a job might already be working for you or your company. The best part is that you already know their work habits and attitude.

3. Offer referral bonuses to current employees. In a tightening skills market, offering such bonuses will increase the chance of locating qualified applicants.

4. Don't hesitate to rehire former employees. Keep in touch with the good ones; even if they don't return to your company, they may have excellent colleagues to recommend. Also, don't rule out family members of persons already employed.

5. Make effective use of personnel services firms. Especially use those that specialize in candidates in the particular disciplines you need.

6. Be creative in your help-wanted advertising, not only in preparing it but in choosing the appropriate media as well.

PAY ATTENTION TO JOB DESCRIPTIONS

1. Accurately define the jobs you're looking to fill.

2. Don't immediately fill a vacancy created when an employee leaves. It may not have to be filled at all; perhaps it can be combined with another position, or handled by two existing employees with the use of qualified temporary help for peak workloads.

RESUMES: READ BETWEEN THE LINES

1. Assume that if you don't see clear indications of particular attributes on a resume, the applicant probably doesn't possess them.

2. Start at the end. Most candidates put the least flattering information there.

3. Be wary of functional resumes that describe experience and qualifications without corresponding dates of employment.

4. Look for profit-mindedness. Does the candidate appreciate the fact that companies exist to make money? How many times does the candidate point to accomplishments that directly benefitted the employer?

5. Glean actual work experience from superfluous information. A puffed-up resume often contains excessive personal trivia (sports interests, children's accomplishments, hobbies, etc.) that may indicate that the candidate lacks substantive experience and skills.

INTERVIEW SMART

There are dozens of questions to be asked of candidates, depending on the job to be filled and the interviewer's personal style and needs. However, here are eight basic questions to be asked of job candidates, prefaced by, "Please answer my questions the way you think your references will answer them when they're contacted." This makes it clear that you will really check references. It may cause the job candidate to withdraw, but that will be a blessing in disguise.

1. "Why are you looking to change jobs?" If the candidate bad-mouths a current or past employer, think twice.

2. "What did you like best about your last job?" A candidate who can't give you a thoughtful answer might not think beyond the basic mechanics of a job.

3. "If you could have made improvements in your last job, what would they have been?" The answer can be a useful barometer of a candidate's creativity.

4. "Who was the most interesting customer or client you dealt with in your last job?" (Or, "What has been the most interesting job or project so far in your career?") The reasons given are more important than the nature of the project and can provide valuable insight into the candidate's motivations.

5. "Describe the best person who ever worked for or with you." Answers can uncover something about the candidate's personality as well as the qualities he or she admires.

6. "What kind of people annoy you the most?" Frequently, annoying traits that candidates mention do not apply to themselves.

7. "Describe emergencies or unexpected assignments that forced you to reschedule your work time." This will elicit more pro-

ductive answers than the yes-or-no question, "Are you willing to work extra hours when the situation calls for it?"

8. "What assistance would you need from us to help you get off to a good start?" Look for balance in the answers. A candidate who comes up with a reasons list demonstrates a good sense of planning and organization. Needing too much help or, at the other extreme, no help at all doesn't strike the desired balance.

Schedule the right amount of time for each interview, and know when and how to end them. Here are some tips:

1. Set a time limit at the beginning. Have a clock visible and let the candidate know at the start roughly how long you'll be together.
2. Cue the candidate when the interview is nearing its end. If you're using pencil and paper, put the pencil down and push the paper aside, or look at your watch and refer to another appointment.
3. End on the appropriate note, depending on whether the candidate is a definite contender, a "maybe," or out of the running.

One of the biggest problems interviewers have is keeping track of myriad candidates. (Remember, the first candidates interviewed from a large field of applicants, even if outstanding, are often forgotten and not hired.) Relying on memory is risky and inefficient. Make careful notes and establish an informal rating system that includes experience, education, apparent intelligence, professional appearance, and communication skills. Also attempt to evaluate and rank each candidate's less tangible qualities, such as motivation and enthusiasm.

A final tip on interviewing: Have leading job candidates come into contact with several levels of management, but don't hire by committee. Committees often end up hiring a "compromise candidate," one who neither completely pleases nor offends anyone on the committee. In most cases, this will not be the best person for the job.

CHECK REFERENCES

There are basically two ways to handle references: thoroughly or not at all. Here are five points worth bearing in mind for those who'll take the thorough approach:

1. Check the references of candidates who will report directly to you. Other managers should do the same.

2. Don't delay. Begin your investigation as soon as the candidate has given you permission. The longer you wait to hire, the greater the risk of losing the candidate.

3. Pay little attention to written references given to you by the candidate, but by all means use them as springboards for additional reference checking.

4. Seek references not provided by the candidate. Call the candidate's previous employer and ask for somebody other than the individual whose name you've been given, or ask that person to suggest someone else who knows the candidate and his or her work. Network references this way until a clear picture of the person has emerged.

5. For high-level jobs, conduct as many reference checks in person as possible. Use the phone as a second approach. The mail is rarely productive when checking references.

LAND THE WINNER

The better the candidate, the more in demand he or she is likely to be. When you believe you've found the right person, take immediate action.

1. Don't delay the offer. If the candidate is unemployed, you can always hire contingent on references checking out.

2. Set an early start date. The longer the time between job offer and start date, the greater the risk of losing the chosen candidate to another employer.

AFTER THE HIRE: LET YOUR PEOPLE KNOW THEY COUNT

1. Do something special for special people. Encourage good performance by acknowledging it. Praise is often as good as a raise.

2. Bestow new titles. Employees appreciate them, and they don't necessarily cost anything.

3. Be kind and courteous.

4. Be fair. Employees respect a well-managed tight ship as long as the basic rules and regulations apply to everyone.

KEEP YOUR EMPLOYEES INVOLVED

1. Establish and nurture that valuable team feeling, and reward teams as well as individual achievement.

2. Be receptive to suggestions. Don't just wait for them to be offered. Actively encourage them every day.

3. Reward risk as well as results. Applaud smart risk taking, even if it fails. Give employees enough latitude to achieve their full potential.

4. Use in-house newsletters to boost morale. Look beyond the typical employee newsletter for ways to enhance the communications between management and staff.

5. Make meetings meaningful. Schedule them only when there's a specific need. Holding meetings for the sake of holding meetings wastes everyone's time and particularly annoys achievers.

6. Toot the company's horn. Employees like working for a winner. Be sure all employees are informed of the company's accomplishments. Your employees should be your first and primary audience for public relations and should be treated like a customer.

KEEP THE COMPENSATION PACKAGE COMPETITIVE

1. Consider paying slightly above the prevailing salary range, if possible. When employees work for less than the job market is paying, it may cost your company more in the long run. Whatever extra it costs in the short run will pay handsome dividends later by encouraging employees to volunteer for extra work, and will keep them from jumping to competitors.

2. Be flexible. No single compensation policy can meet the needs of all employees.

3. Establish an equitable system of raises. In well-run companies, *most* people don't have to ask for raises. Their employees know what to expect—and when to expect it—because of their awareness that these companies value and reward performance, ingenuity, loyalty, and dedication.

4. Say "no" with grace. Be willing to admit mistakes. Listen. Communicate. Encourage a sense of humor, even when the joke's on you.

HOW TO KEEP GOOD EMPLOYEES

Companies that have been successful in retaining good employees report the following factors, listed in order of importance, as playing a pivotal role in their success.

1. Competitive salaries and benefits
2. Open communication
3. Good work environment
4. Incentive programs
5. Periodic review/counseling
6. Promotions/better job in the department or another division
7. Stock options
8. Deferred compensation
9. Management-by-objective programs
10. A fair and meaningful employment contract
11. Savings and matching programs
12. Profit sharing

LITTLE THINGS MEAN A LOT

Here is a list of benefits that cost little or nothing:

1. Praise
2. Personal notes for achievements
3. Desirable assignments
4. Public recognition
5. Titles
6. Small gifts for special occasions (e.g., birthdays, weddings)
7. Tickets to sporting events and shows
8. Temporary help or assistance
9. Free coffee and snacks
10. Facilities for heating lunch
11. A pleasant work environment

AN EMPLOYEE MIGHT BE LOOKING FOR ANOTHER JOB IF:

1. There's a noticeable change in attitude, especially if it shifts from active to passive
2. There's less communication
3. Lunch hours become longer
4. Absences increase
5. There are more personal phone calls than usual
6. Grooming and dress suddenly improve
7. A desk becomes neater
8. There's a change in vacation patterns
9. Work is no longer taken home

WHAT TO DO ABOUT AN EMPLOYEE WHO IS JOB HUNTING

1. Be direct. Ask if the employee is looking to work elsewhere.
2. Try to keep the good ones, but resist making a counteroffer; employees rarely stay more than a year after accepting one.
3. Recognize that some turnover is positive; it weeds out the less competent and buoys the morale of others.
4. Leave the door open. If the employee is valuable, extend the opportunity to return if the new position doesn't work out.
5. Keep things amicable.

WHEN YOU HAVE TO FIRE SOMEONE

1. Know that most employees who are fired expect it.
2. Have adequate cause, and document it.
3. Don't pass the buck. Termination should be handled directly by the highest authority the employee deals with on a regular basis and should be done in person, face-to-face—no pink slips in the mail, no phone calls.
4. Analyze honestly what went wrong.
5. Have all necessary separation information on hand.

6. Don't drag it out.

7. Be tactful and truthful.

8. Be prudent in what you say to other employees.

SUMMING UP

Ultimately, when a company experiences frequent employee turnover, the result is that the best employees leave while the less valuable ones remain, a situation destined to place that company in a difficult competitive position.

No company, large or small, need find itself in such a tenuous and undesirable position. To avoid it, two things must remain uppermost in mind:

1. Hire smart to begin with.

2. Respect and reward those "smart" hires.

I hope that *Finding, Hiring, and Keeping the Best Employees* not only has provided some of the nuts-and-bolts of achieving this end, but also has encouraged its readers to address the hiring and retention process as a critically important function of management.

INDEX

If you're not looking here, you're hardly looking.

There are lots of publications you can turn to when you're looking for a job. But in today's tough job market, you need the National Business Employment Weekly. It not only lists hundreds of high-paying jobs available now at major corporations all across the country, it also gives you valuable strategies and advice to help you land one of those jobs. NBEW is a Wall Street Journal publication. It's the leading national job-search and career guidance publication and has been for over ten years. Pick it up at your newsstand today. Or get the next 12 issues delivered first class for just $52 by calling toll-free…

800-367-9600

National Business Employment Weekly

If you're not looking here, you're hardly looking.